through the   your feet

A walking & field guide to Alonnisos and the
surrounding islands of the Marine Park

Second Edition

By
Chris Browne

Published by *Travelleur*

First published in 2013 by

Travelleur

96 Thorpes Avenue
Denby Dale
Huddersfield HD8 8TB
UK

© Chris Browne 2013

ISBN 978-0-9576115-0-4

Second Edition

Printed and bound by in Great Britain by
CPI Group (UK) Ltd, Croyden CRO 4YY

The author has walked and researched all the routes for this guide, but no responsibility can be accepted for any unforeseen circumstances encountered whilst following them. However, should you have any problems or find material changes to the walks the publisher would be grateful for this information.

With fond memories of my dear brother Mick

My thanks to all those who helped me with
this second edition of "souls".

Chris' wife Julia is the founder of the Alonnisos Society for Animal
Protection (ASAP), the aim of which is the promotion of respect for pets,
stray animals, the natural environment and the raising of public
awareness with respect to their care. More information and membership
details are available at www.asap-animalz.org. Julia is the author of 'An
insider's guide to Alonnisos', also published by Travelleur.

"Take only photographs, leave only footprints, kill only time"

Contents

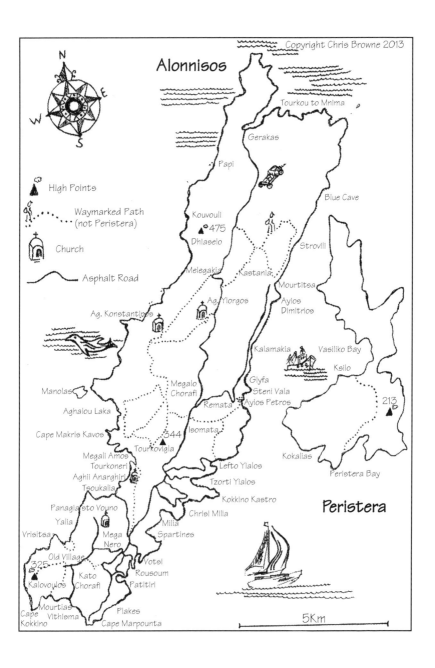

Copyright Chris Browne 2013

Alonnisos

N
W E
S

High Points

Waymarked Path
(not Peristera)

Church

Asphalt Road

Tourkou to Mnima

Gerakas

Papi

Blue Cave

Kouvouli
▲ 475
Dhiaselo

Strovili

Melegakia
Kastania

Mourtitsa

Ag. Yiorgos
Ayios
Dimitrios

Ag. Konstantinos

Kalamakia
Vasiliko Bay

Ksilo

Manolas

Megalo
Chorafi
Glyfa
Steni Vala

213

Aghalou Laka
Remata
Ayios Petros

Cape Makris Kavos
Isomata

344
Tourkovigla
Kokalias

Megali Amos
Tourkoneri
Lefto Yialos
Peristera Bay

Aghii Anarghiri
Tsoukalia
Tzorti Yialos

Kokkino Kastro

Panagia sto Vouno
Milia
Chrisi Milia

Peristera

Yalia
Mega
Nero
Spartines

Vrisitsa

Old Village
Votsi

325
Kato
Chorafi
Rousoum
Patitiri

Kalovoulos

Mourtias
Cape
Vithisma
Plakes

Kokkino
Cape Marpounta

5Km

Introduction

For such a small island (23km x 3km) Alonnisos has a wide variety of terrain, ranging from relatively easy walks along forest trails and through unspoilt olive and almond groves, to a boulder strewn remote gorge or a taxing climb to the high point of the island in the north.

From the pine forests in the south, to the wild macchia vegetation of the north and a coastline dotted with small blue coves and white pebble beaches the island is abundant in natural beauty. In spring the profusion of wild flowers and herbs provide an explosion of colour and fragrance, which can only really be appreciated on foot.

Walking along the routes covered in this book gives you a unique insight into life on the island, both as it is today and as it was in years gone by. Perhaps on the "Across the Centre of the Island" walk, along the traditional old footpath from Melegakia in the north to the church of Ayios Konstantinos, over the "aloni" (threshing floor) and past the "lakka" (small wheat fields), you will get a glimpse of life as it used to be.

Somewhere on your travels you are sure to bump into a shepherd, the resin collector, an old woman collecting her horta (wild greens) or perhaps someone leaving an offering at one of the many roadside shrines. If you do then a cheery greeting of "Yassas" will almost always get you a reply.

By walking here you help to keep open the network of footpaths for others to use and enjoy. It is also possible to walk on the deserted islands of the marine park, an unforgettable experience.

I hope this book helps you to enjoy the walking, swimming and snorkelling on Alonnisos and the surrounding islands. Any comments you may have about this book would be welcome by email to alonnisoswalks@yahoo.co.uk

Chris Browne, Alonnisos 2013

How to use this book

Walk Descriptions

Every walk is of course entirely different when made in April/May than in say September, but no less enjoyable. Visiting Alonnisos out of season for walking can be a very rewarding experience too. Most of the walks have a "main route" and then several options. I have got no less pleasure from doing a particular walk for the umpteenth time than for the first time, particularly when it involved exploring a new option or diversion. I hope that you will find this useful, perhaps when you visit the island again and want to make your walk that little bit different.

The maps are intended to be used as a guide in conjunction with the written description of each walk. Please remember that walking routes may change without warning for a variety of reasons. ***Text in bold italics like this is additional information or a short diversion,*** and major options to a walk are included at the end of the main route description.

The description of each walk starts with information on route, distance, average time with no stops, terrain, beach stops, beach tavernas and footwear/clothing. Please also read "what to take and wear". Times are based on an average walking speed of 3km/2miles per hour. A useful companion to this book is the "Anavasi" hiking map of Alonnisos usually available locally on Alonnisos.

Most of the waymarked footpaths have a short section of paved path at each end and many of the routes are now marked by paint spots, though not always the same colour! Be aware that land boundaries are also marked by paint splodges and some lovely wide looking forest paths come to an abrupt end where the resin collector who uses the path got fed up!

Please ensure you read the entire description of the walk you plan to do before setting off, and please respect the **NO SMOKING** and **NO FIRES** ban when in wooded areas.

What to take and wear

Day pack, picnic if required, water bottle (1.5L for each person is recommended), high SPF sun cream, insect bite stick, sun-hat, comfortable and suitable footwear, zip-offs or lightweight trousers to put on over your shorts in case of heavy undergrowth, swimwear and a shirt to cover shoulders and neck to give protection from the sun and the straps on your day pack. Due to the high temperatures that can be expected it is recommended to walk early or late in the day and avoid walking in the middle of the day. You can plan most walks to include a refreshing lunch time swim stop.

Please Note: many of the walks are in remote areas away from medical assistance. You should therefore be in good health and reasonably fit. If you have a mobile phone take it with you but be aware that large areas of Alonnisos, particularly the north, do not have mobile phone coverage. If you need to summon assistance from a non Greek phone you must dial 0030 before the number you require.

ALL WALKS ARE UNDERTAKEN AT YOUR OWN RISK

Useful Phone Numbers:

Health Centre: 24240 65208 (during the season there is usually a dentist here)

Doctor on call mobile: 6932 489883

Dentist: 24240 65616 Mobile: 6937 231812

Pharmacies 24240 65540 & 66096 Mobile: 6944 580044

Police: 24240 65205

Port Police: 24240 65595

Fire Brigade: 24240 65199

Taxis: 6978881360 & 6976221441

Place Names

English	Greek
Alonnisos	Αλόννησος
Sporades	Σποράδες
Ayios Dimitrios	Άγιος Δημήτριος
Ayios Petros	Άγιος Πέτρος
Alonnisos Old Village	Αλόννησος (Παλιά Χώρα)
Cape Kokkino (Red Cape)	Κόκκινο Ακρ.
Cape Marpounta	Ακρ. Μαρπούντα
Chrisi Milia (Golden apple tree)	Χρυσή Μηλιά
Dhiaselo	Διάσελο
Kalamakia	Καλαμάκια
Kalovoulos	Καλόβουλος
Kato Chorafi (Lower field)	Κάτω Χωράφι
Kokinokastro (Red castle)	Κοκκινόκαστρο
Koumarorachi (Strawberry tree ridge)	Κουμαρόραχη
Kyra Panagia (The Virgin Mary)	Κύρα Παναγιά
Glyfa	Γλυφά
Gerakas	Γέρακας
Isomata (Flat place)	Ισώματα
Lefto Yialos	Λεφτό Γιαλός
Megali Amos (Big sand)	Μεγάλι Άμος
Meghalos Mourtias (Big myrtle tree)	Μεγάλος Μουρτιάς
Mikros Mourtias (Small myrtle tree)	Μικρός Μουρτιάς
Milia (Apple tree)	Μηλιά
Mourtitsa	Μουρτίτσα

English	Greek
Paliochorafina	Παλιοχωραφίνα
Patitiri	Πατητήρι
Plakes	Πλάκες
Rousoum	Ρουσούμ
Spartines	Σπαρτίνες
Steni Vala (Narrow valley)	Στενή Βάλα
Strovili (eddy- water)	Στροβίλι
Tsoukalia	Τσουκαλιά
Vamvakies	Βαμβακιές
Votsi	Βότση
Vithisma	Βύθισμα
Vrisitsa (small spring)	Βρυσίτσα
Yalia	Γιάλια

Transport for your walks

There is a bus service between Patitiri and the Old Village and Patitiri and Steni Vala. The timetable is displayed on the bus stop at the bottom of the main hill down into Patitiri harbour, opposite the Alkyon hotel and next to the taxi rank. You can ask the bus driver to drop you off along the way and hail him to stop for you.

The taxi drivers will drop you off at the start of a walk and are reliable enough to pick you up from a pre-arranged location at the end of your walk. Make sure you have their mobile phone number though!

There is also a new coach service that runs from Patitiri to various beaches, tickets available from the kiosk next to the port police office.

A Dimitra. Built around old boat diesel engines.

Snorkelling Sites

Here is a small selection of the places I have found to be especially good.

The sea cave just outside Patitiri (see the **Patitiri Coastal Walk**). All along this section of coast is good.

The ferry port turn left along the quay and left again out onto the rocks. There is a ladder down into the sea. Around under the cliff to the left towards Rousoum and across to the rock is good.

Off the mole at Votsi Harbour (see the **South East Coast Walk**). Into the cave and then keep left along the coast. There are two nice pebble beaches along here, some amazing underwater rock formations and on the open sea end of the first headland another great cave you can swim into. A monk seal has been spotted along here many times.

Cape Makris Kavos (see **Across The Centre of the Island Walk**)

Tourkoneri Beach (see the **10 km Marathon Walk**). From Tourkoneri beach swim out and around the coast to the left underneath the church of Aghii Anarghiri.

Shipwreck at Ayios Dimitrios Beach. As you go down the approach road turn left onto the beach. Turn left when on the beach and walk back towards the main coastline. Look for a solitary tree at the back of the beach on your left. Enter the sea here, swim out about 10m, then turn right and swim parallel to the beach. You are looking for what appears to be a lot of very dark green rocks on the sea floor. This is the wreck and it lies roughly parallel to the beach with the stern towards the main coastline. When you find it the prow is at about 10m and bits of the wooden hull are still visible here. The green stones are lumps of rough bronze and very heavy. The wreck is probably no more than 100 years old. Please do not remove items from the wreck. Swimming north along the coast from here is also good for a variety of marine life.

Kokalias hole. On the southern end of Peristera island directly opposite Lefto Yialos beach on Alonnisos, is the small cove of Kokalias. At the back of the cove is a lovely small pebble beach at the foot of an olive grove which makes a fantastic picnic spot. Swim out from the beach and keep tight to the coastline on your right. You will swim around a right hand bend. Swim straight ahead towards the facing coast and keep a sharp lookout below you. You will see a black shadow on the sea floor. This is the hole and the opening is at about 5m depth. If you are a good diver you can, with care, swim down into the hole, which continues down out of sight. There are normally many fish around here.

Ayios Yorgos rock holes. Ayios Yorgos is the larger of the two small islets between Alonnisos & Skopelos. The stretch of sea between Alonnisos & Ayios Yorgos is notoriously fickle so only make this trip in your own boat if the weather is set calm. Megalos Mourtias beach is the nearest place to set off from. As you approach Ayios Yorgos you will see a small beach. Head for this. On the left side as you approach there is an unusual corridor in the rock face through which you can swim. On the right side you can walk around the rocky coast and you will find three places where there are large openings down to the sea below. You can dive down and swim out to the open sea from all of these. There are many Eleonora's falcons which nest on the high cliffs here. It is also possible to walk up to the little church and ruined monastery on this island. As you leave the beach turn right and go around the side of the island towards Skopelos. On your right you will see the small white church above you, surrounded by the stone remains of the monastery. There is a small jetty below.

The sunken city of Psathoura. If you are lucky enough to get to this, the most remote of the Marine Park islands, you may like to know where the only visible underwater remains are actually located. As you approach the beach of Mandraki on Psathoura from the direction of Kyra Panagia, you will see a rocky islet off to the right. Towards the north end of the islet on the side facing you is where the visible remains are. These include stone steps and a wellhead. Around the east side of the island there is also a large relatively modern shipwreck and, according to local legend, the remains of a WWII German fighter plane. Along the back of Mandraki beach you will see many rare white sea lilies.

Skantzoura & Dio Adelphi (see Skantzoura Island Walk). I think the site on the "Big Brother" is the best around. There is a tiny rocky islet just at the entrance to the small cove of "Ostria" on the right. The inner side is shallow, the outer very deep. The variety and abundance of fish here is amazing.

Near Plakes beach; the view to the islands of the "Two Brothers" (Dio Adelphia)

Flora and Fauna

The National Marine Park of Alonnisos was established in 1983 and was the first to be founded in Greece. Although the main objective of the park is the protection of the endangered monk seal, it also hosts a number of rare species of wildlife and is rich in both flora and fauna. There are around 300 species of fish, 80 species of birds, plus reptiles and mammals.

The *Mediterranean Monk Seal* is the world's largest seal species and is the most endangered marine mammal in Europe. It is estimated that the seas around Alonnisos are home to some 60 of these rare animals.

The wildlife on Alonnisos consists of many varieties of birds including raptors and game birds; reptiles such as tortoise, snakes and lizards; and mammals such as hedgehogs and rabbits.

Birds

Alonnisos is host to a large variety of birds. These range from swallows, shrike, house martins, cuckoos, alpine swifts, hooded crows and ravens, to the exotic Bonelli's eagle and bee-eaters. At night time if you hear what sounds like a frog or toad, it's probably a nightjar, and the double high pitched "peep-peep" (which sounds like sonar) will be the little Scops owl. Notable birdlife includes:

*The **Eleonora's Falcon**.* Around 70% of the world breeding population of this endangered falcon is in Greece. Alonnisos and the surrounding islands of the Marine Park are important protected habitats. You can watch their amazing aerial duels with buzzards and hooded crows which come too close to their nesting site. They can be seen

Eleonora's Falcon feeding her chicks

all over Alonnisos and have a distinctive "scri-scri" call and curved wing shape in flight. They nest high up on the cliffs, lay two to three eggs during August and live on small birds and insects which they take in flight. They migrate from Africa to the Mediterranean in the summer.

Audouin's Gull is a very rare sea bird which nests only in the Mediterranean and Aegean. The total population is estimated at 21.500 pairs with 350 to 500 pairs in Greece and 90% of these nesting in the Marine Park. Skantzoura is an important habitat. Smaller than a common gull it has a distinctive red bill with a black tip.

The **Scops Owl:** this small-eared owl with yellow eyes is both nocturnal and incredibly well camouflaged making it difficult to see but its high pitched, sonar-like "peep-peep" whistle, repeated every few seconds, can be heard at night throughout the summer. They can sometimes be spotted at night on top of electricity poles.

The Shag is a marine bird and a vulnerable species. It nests along the rocky coasts and is smaller than the more common cormorant. They both dive deep in the sea to catch the fish on which they live. You will often see them standing on the rocks along the coast, holding up their wings.

Corey's *and* **Manx Shearwaters** can be spotted around the coast of Alonnisos. If you go on a boat trip, or just look out to sea from the shore in the summer, you will usually see large numbers of birds gliding impossibly close to the waves.

The **Hoopoe** visits Alonnisos both in spring and early autumn. These multi-coloured birds have a crest on their heads which they raise when on the ground. When in flight they appear as a flash of black, yellow and white. Vouno is a good place to see them.

Reptiles

Lizards and geckos are to be seen everywhere on Alonnisos. The most common reptiles are the **wall lizards** which are a variety of greens and browns in colour. Of an evening the **Turkish geckos** (which are a translucent orange) can be seen feasting on flies and moths and it is possible see them change colour to grey as they fill up. You may also be lucky enough to see the relatively rare **emerald lizard**, normally scuttling across the road. They can be up to a foot long and are a vivid emerald green.

There are **snakes** on the island but most of these are non-poisonous. The large dark brown and green ones are either harmless **grass snakes** or **whip snakes** which are generally very keen on avoiding humans: probably your only contact with one will be when you hear it disappearing into the undergrowth in an attempt to get out of your way.

However there are two species of **viper**, the **common** and **horn nosed**, and they are both venomous. They are typically quite short and have a diamond pattern on their back. It is not a good idea to poke around in stone walls as this is where they like to relax. These are also shy but, whereas the grass snakes will slither away when they sense something approaching, adders tend to freeze. The answer is to watch where you put your feet when walking through the undergrowth and make a lot of noise. An adder bite will not prove fatal, unless there is some underlying medical condition, but may cause some unpleasant side effects such as severe headache and muscle pains. If bitten keep calm, avoid exertion and seek medical advice immediately. Do not apply tourniquets or try to suck the poison from the wound. Many reptiles harbour salmonella bacteria, so should be handled cautiously (or preferably not at all). This applies particularly to **tortoises**.

Mammals

If you walk out after dusk you will almost certainly see **bats** swooping after insects. They are a protected species and roost mainly in caves. They seem to be particularly fond of carob trees, probably due to the amount of insects there. Bats will  consume several thousand insects every night.

As there are no natural predators there is also a large **rabbit** population.

There are also still several large **goat herds** and a few smaller herds of sheep towards the north of Alonnisos.

Butterflies, Moths and Insects

Alonnisos is home to a variety of butterflies including Swallowtails, the Double Tailed Pasha, Brimstones and Red Admirals. Many people wonder what the tiny hummingbird like insect is that they see over the summer. This is the **Hummingbird Hawk Moth** and is commonly seen during daylight hours hovering around flowers, particularly geraniums, and sucking their nectar whilst in flight.

You might also see the **Giant Peacock Moth**, the largest moth in Europe and also known as the Giant Emperor Moth or Viennese Emperor.

You may see nests hanging in the pine trees that look like weaver birds' nests. These are the nests of the **pine processionary caterpillar**. In addition to being very destructive to pine trees, they also have highly irritating hairs which, if touched (either directly or indirectly), will introduce a toxin causing skin welts and immense local irritation probably requiring antihistamine treatment. These little beasts are only in evidence early in the year and can be seen walking nose to tail in long lines

In the late 1980s there was a blight on the almond trees, treated with intensive spraying. This had a devastating impact on the **bee** population and industry surrounding them. It is good to note that this industry is now on the increase again and hives can be seen all over the island.

Insects include mantids, ladybirds and, unfortunately, several types of tick. Whenever you return from a walk, particularly if you have been near goats, then check yourself for ticks.

If you decide to sleep on or near a beach it's wise to use insect repellent to guard against being bitten by **sandflies**. These may spread a protozoal infection called leishmaniasis (Kala-azar) which is very difficult to treat. In early summer you also have to be aware of the green, goggle-eyed **deer fly**. These large flies have an incredibly irritating bite and are particularly attracted to wet skin, so it's wise to dry yourself after swimming.

Rarely, **scorpions** may be seen. Avoid walking around in bare feet and shake out clothes and shoes before putting them on. If you should be stung, seek medical attention immediately.

Marine Life

No visit to Alonnisos would be complete without seeing **dolphin**. If you go out on a boat trip you have a very good chance of spotting them, particularly during early summer. It is also common to see them from the shore around Cape Marpounta, off Megalos Mourtias

beach below the Old Village and Glyfa beach near Steni Vala. It is possible to see **Common, Striped** and **Bottle Nosed dolphins**.

A variety of **urchins** are to be found in rocky areas of the sea-shore. I would recommend being careful where you put your hands and wearing beach shoes when swimming. If you touch an urchin and the spines become embedded in your flesh please resist the urge to prod, poke or pick at them to get them out. By doing this you risk infection. If you leave them, local inflammation will push the spines out naturally within a couple of days.

Periodically there are **jelly-fish** in the sea (fortunately no man-of-war species): most frequently these are the transparent blob kind which are harmless, but sometimes there may be much larger, yellowish jelly-fish of the Cassiopeia species. If you should be stung by a jelly-fish or a flying insect such as a wasp or hornet, application of a dilute acid such as vinegar or lemon juice will relieve the pain. I have it on good authority that urine also works, but have not tried this myself.

Stingrays and **skates** frequent bays with sandy bottoms where they can bury themselves in the sand and then lie in wait for the eager paddler to tread on them. They are shy creatures but will lash out with their tails if trodden on. This can be very painful, so it is wise to make your presence known in advance by splashing around when entering the water.

Flowers

Although early spring is a particularly good time for flora on Alonnisos, a number of interesting species can be found throughout the year. As well as the flowers mentioned below there are many types of lily, iris, cyclamen and poppy. From the ground-covering Friar's cowl to the elegant gladioli and roadside acanthus, there is always something for those keen on flora.

Alonnisos is home to a wide variety of **orchid species** including many types of **bee orchid** and other **Ophrys orchids**. They can be spotted from as early as late January and the various species are about for much of the year and in a variety of habitats from olive groves and rocky slopes to shaded forests.

The tall (up to 1.5m), single-stemmed flowers which rise from very large bulbs in late summer are **sea squills** (these can be confused with the asphodels which flower in late spring and also cover the rocky slopes of Alonnisos but which are multi-branched at the top). In the winter, after the flower of the sea squill dies, the broad, pointed leaves (up to 60cm tall) sprout from the bulb. These plants are so numerous because they are poisonous to the goats which graze the slopes of Alonnisos. The bulbs have been used medicinally for humans since ancient times for the treatment of heart disease, coughs and chapped feet! A dry bulb will survive for seven years and still put out new leaves. For this reason it became a fertility symbol and is still hung outside some Greek houses at New Year.

In early summer you may spot some very unusual-looking tiny red and white plants underneath the cistus. This is **Cytinus rubra.** It is a parasite which contains no chlorophyll and lives on the roots of the cistus. On Alonnisos they can be found in the forests near to Aghii Anarghiri and on the walk up from Aghalou Lakka.

A widespread evergreen shrub which may also catch your eye is **shrubby globularia** with its bright blue flower clusters at the end of multi-branched stems.

A very unassuming flower is one of the types of **false dittany** on the island. It is widespead all over Alonnisos and its large green to yellow calyx is often mistaken for the flower which is actually purple and, although fairly insignificant, is a great draw for insects. The interesting fact about this plant is that once the seed vessels are dried they are still used today as floating wicks in the roadside shrines and can even be bought for this purpose in the women's co-operative shop in Patitiri.

Squirting Cucumbers grow anywhere and can be seen under the cliff face on the road towards the main port in Patitiri. They have sprawling stems and yellow flowers. The green hairy fruit explode when ripe and emit a liquid which is strong purgative. It has been used in the treatment of rheumatism, shingles and paralysis **but** the liquid is extremely poisonous.

Another rare and beautiful plant to see if you get the chance is the **sea lily** or **sea daffodil** *(Pancratium maritinum)*. In order to see this, however, you would have to visit the coastal dunes of Psathoura Island in July/ August.

Common Herbs

Thyme is an aromatic low shrublet found all over the island, particularly on stony ground. It has purplish-pink flowers and is much used by honey bees. As well as its culinary uses, thyme is a source of ethereal oil used in medicine and perfumery. Herbalists believe it has medicinal value. The oil is also used in veterinary medicine.

Giant Fennel is commonly seen along road verges and on waste ground. On Alonnisos some of the tallest specimens are around the Mega Nero area. It can grow to 2m tall or more and has bright green feathery leaves and yellow flowers on branched hollow stems. The hollow stems when lit burn very slowly and were therefore used to carry fire over long distances.

Sage is a low shrub with a strong aromatic smell. The most succulent examples are in shaded forest areas and particularly along the edges of the gorge walk. Its dried leaves are commonly used to make a medicinal tea, good for everything from a sore throat to a stomach upset. The tea is sometimes sold in Greek cafés and in the supermarkets under the name "faskomelo".

Sage and Wild Garlic in the forest near Aghii Anarghiri

16

One of the most common herbs growing on Alonnisos, and one you are most likely to come across in tavernas, is **oregano**. It is the herb scattered over the feta in Greek salad and on pork chops amongst other things. This is best collected when in flower. In the supermarket closest to the big pine tree on the main road in Patitiri you can often "bulk buy" plastic bags of wonderful, local oregano very cheaply.

Samphire is known locally as "kritama". It is found on rocks close to the sea and traditionally served pickled with ouzo, tsipouro and octopus. Like many of the dried herbs and preserved fruit, "kritama" can be bought in the Ikos women's co-operative in Patitiri.

Trees

The **Carob Tree (Ceratonia)** has long, leathery brown pods hanging from its branches. The pods have been used as a food source for humans throughout hard times but are now used to feed the island's many goats. In the past they were also used to feed the island's cattle. If you open up a pod you will notice that all the seeds are a uniform size. These seeds were used as the "carat" weight for jewellers throughout the world. The word "carat" derives from the Arabian "kirat" which, in turn, comes from the Greek name for the tree "keratian".

The **Myrtle tree (Myrtus communis)** can be found in many places on Alonnisos but you are sure to see it if you walk up the Old Donkey Track. The Greek name for this tree is *myrtia* and it is this that the beaches of Mourtias are named after ("megalos" meaning big and "mikros" meaning small). Myrtle is a classical symbol of love and wreaths of it are still used in wedding ceremonies. The berries can be fermented into an alcoholic drink. Many remedies are based on myrtle and have been ever since the time of Dioscorides.

The **Strawberry Tree (Arbutus unendo)** is a fairly common tree on Alonnisos. There are only a few examples of the **Eastern Strawberry Tree (Arbutus andrachne)** which is very distinctive due to the peeling, reddish bark which can be quite spectacular at times. The leaves of the Eastern Strawberry tree are untoothed and the flowers erect. There are good examples of the Eastern Strawberry tree at Megalo Chorafi and the later section of the walk from Ayios Konstantinos to Megalo Chorafi. See the "Across the Centre of the Island" walk. The Strawberry Tree Arbutus unendo is very common on Alonnisos. Indeed the area around the beginning of the gorge is called Koumarorachi or "Strawberry Tree Ridge", after its Greek name "Koumaria". Despite its name the attractive edible fruit tastes nothing like strawberries. In fact they are quite bland and full of seeds. The word "unendo" means "eat one" which would suggest you wouldn't want to eat more! The fruit are sometimes used to make a brandy -like liqueur and the wood is used to make high quality charcoal and flutes.

The **Judas Tree (Cercis siliquastrum)** has very distinctive pea-like flowers which appear in March and April and are followed by heart-shaped leaves. Later long purple pods appear which contain the peas. Legend has it that this is the tree from which Judas Iscariot hanged himself after denouncing Christ. The story continues that the flowers (pods) were originally pale and blushed pink with shame after that event. The flower buds, though slightly acidic, are sometimes added to salads.

Good examples of the Judas tree can be seen above the main road as you approach the Old Village, (see the "Old Village and Beyond" walk), and the early part of the Gorge Walk from the church of Ayios Yorgos.

Judas Tree in bloom

18

Sunset Walks

There are many places on Alonnisos to enjoy the sunset but here are a few special places.

Behind the hill of Vouno as described in the 4 Churches Walk "optional circuit around the hill of Vouno". From Patitiri the quickest route is up the old donkey track (path number 4). Turn right along the dirt road which crosses it near the top, right again at the asphalt road and left at the *OTE turn* beneath the Sunset Café. Then follow the walk instructions.

Kalovoulos Peak as described in the Old Village and Beyond Walk.

The Old Village: go past the cemetery and take the first right turn. Continue to the end of the road.

Church of Aghii Anaghiri see the 10 km Marathon Walk.

The Sunset Café near the *OTE turn* for a little luxury!

View from the south west coast of Alonnisos, looking at Skopelos

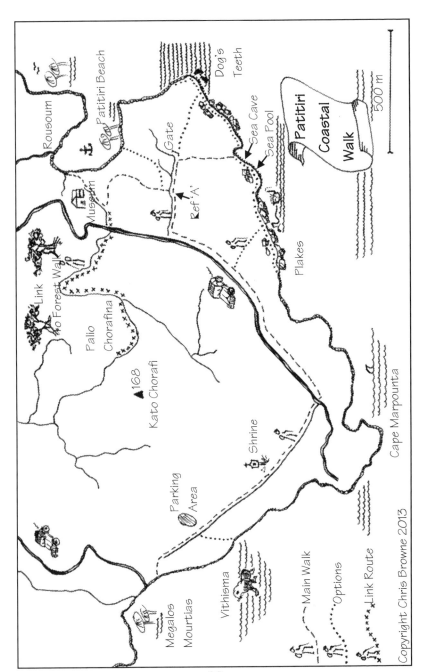

Rousoum

Patitiri Beach

Dog's Teeth

Sea Cave

Gate

Sea Pool

Patitiri
Coastal
Walk

500 m

Museum

Ref 'A'

Plakes

Link

to Forest Walk

Palio
Chorafina

▲168
Kato Chorafi

Shrine

Parking
Area

Cape Marpounta

Megalos
Mourtias

Vithisma

—— Main Walk

· · · · · Options

x—x—x Link Route

Copyright Chris Browne 2013

20

Patitiri Coastal Walk

Main Route: *Patitiri Harbour Beach - Museum - Flakes Beach - Vithisma Beach - Megalos Mourtias Beach*

Includes Sea Cave Option

Main Route Distance: *4 kms*

Time: *2 hours without stops*

Swim stop: *Yes lots!*

Taverna: *Yes at Megalos Mourtias*

Walking shoes recommended. Shorts ok, take swimwear and snorkelling gear.

This walk will show you the extreme south east coastline of Alonnisos. You will be able to swim inside a sea cave and find many secluded spots on the rocks to relax. The walking is easy on established paths except for the steep descent to Vithisma beach. A morning start from Patitiri would allow you plenty of time to explore along this route and then perhaps enjoy a swim and lunch in the excellent taverna Megalos Mourtias with Yianni & Ria.

With your back to the sea in Patitiri take the path off to the left which passes first through the Archipelago ouzeri (no stopping!) and then along past cafés and shops with Patitiri beach immediately on your left. At the end the path turns into steps and at the top you come out almost directly opposite the museum (the museum is owned by Kostas and Angela Mavrikis, who also own the "Ikarus" minimarket and café in Steni Vala. It has many wonderful exhibits and a roof-top café with a stunning view across the harbour). Turn left and go up the steep concrete road past the defunct hotel Galaxy on the left. At the top the road bears sharply right*, on the left there is a small driveway. Just to the right of this a small concrete path going up into the forest.

To link across to the Forest Walk follow the road around this sharp right turn* until it meets the asphalt road and then turn left. You will quickly come to a junction going off to the right signposted Paliochorafina and Nereides Hotel. Take this right turn and you will come to the Neriedes Hotel on the left. Turn left immediately before the hotel to join the Forest Walk.

Take this path up and through the forest behind the Galaxy hotel.

If you wish to visit the beach on the far side of Patitiri harbour then follow this path and keep to the left, then turn left again where you join a dirt road. You will soon come to a path on the left just next to a driveway to a house. This path leads to the small beach.

After about 100m you will see a path off to the right. Take this path and you will come to a dirt road where you turn left. **This is reference point A.**

Go straight ahead and as the road bears around to the left, go straight ahead on a small road between the pine trees. After about 50m as the road bears left there is a wide gate directly in front of you with a sign in Greek and English asking you to close the gate behind you.

If you go through the gate and follow the path straight ahead, with a cottage on your left, you will come down to the rocks on the outside of Patitiri harbour. These rocks are known locally as the "Dog's Teeth". You can explore this lovely section of rocky coastline.

As you approach the gate there are two turnings into the forest on the right, one about half way to the gate and one immediately before the gate. Take the first path and follow it more or less straight ahead through the pine trees and then turn left where it joins another path. After about 50m you will come to what appears to be a dead end and be looking down to your left at a small cove. To the right is a small path*, normally quite overgrown but only for about 20m. The cove to the left has a great sea cave which you can swim or snorkel into. Walk carefully down to the left and onto the rocks at the narrowest part of the cove. As you swim out towards the open sea look on your right hand side for a small inverted V in the rock face at sea level. When the sea is calm and being careful of your head you can duck down under and through here and swim along inside the cave. There is also a hole in the top of the rock face down into the cave. This whole stretch of the coastline is good for snorkelling.

The pool and coastal route to Plakes beach. If you take the small path off to the right you will come to a lovely spot where the sea comes through a narrow gap in the rocks and forms a shallow pool. All around here you can see wild capers and kritama (samphire) growing on the rocks and there is plenty of shade from the pine trees.*

As you stand in the shade of the pines looking down into the pool it is possible to find your way down to the right, across the back of the small beach, and up and around the other side. Once here you can continue all the way along the coastline to the beach of Plakes. The rocks along here are fairly flat and there are some lovely swimming & snorkelling spots.

Return to reference point A and continue up the dirt road straight past the turning on the right you came out of earlier. You will meet the asphalt road where there is a sign to the "Faros" taverna (long since closed).

Turn left and follow the road. You will soon come to a fenced-in area on the left. Immediately before the fence is a small footpath marked with a spot of paint which takes you down to the rocky coast. There is a large pine tree at the end of the path, just behind the rocks, for shade. Plakes beach is just a few metres to your right and is several metres below the rocks you walk on. The beach is narrow with large stones and not very comfortable. You can walk a little bit further along the coast past the beach but you will then come to a dead end. Return to the asphalt road and turn left. Continue until you come to a dirt road going off to your right. Go right here (straight ahead only takes you to the Marpounta Club, an Italian resort hotel: you'll probably hear the noise at some point!). Follow this road along past a memorial plaque up in the trees to the right.

The inscription reads "Here Georgios Andreas Tsoumas accidentally fell and was saved by Germans in the year 1944. The Saints be praised".

You will come to a small flat parking area on the right just before the road starts dropping sharply towards the end of the road and Megalos Mourtias beach. The path down to Vithisma beach is opposite here on the left, the beach name has now been painted on a nearby telegraph pole.

If you do not wish to visit Vithisma beach then keep straight on to Megalos Mourtias beach. See below.*

Take this path down and turn right at the bottom to Vithisma beach. Return back up to the road and turn left.

* Follow the road around until the end where you come to a large gate in front of you across the driveway to a house. Turn left down the path onto Megalos Mourtias beach, past Yianni and Ria's taverna on the right.

You can return to Patitiri the same way or relax in one of the tavernas and ask them to call you a taxi.

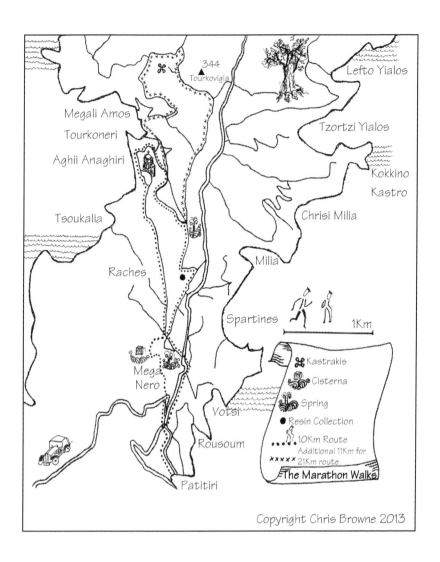

Lefto Yialos

Megali Amos

Tourkoneri

Aghii Anaghiri

Tsoukalia

344
Tourkovigla

Tzortzi Yialos

Kokkino
Kastro

Chrisi Milia

Raches

Milia

Spartines

1Km

Mega
Nero

Kastrakis

Cisterna

Spring

Resin Collection

Votsi

10Km Route
Additional 11Km for
21Km route

The Marathon Walks

Rousoum

Patitiri

Copyright Chris Browne 2013

The 10km Marathon Walk

Main Route: *Patitiri - Mega Nero - Aghii Anarghiri - Tourkoneri Beach - Raches Pine Resin Collection Point - Patitiri*

Time: *3-4 hours without stops*

Swim Stop: *Yes at Tourkoneri beach*

No Tavernas

Walking sandals and shorts are ok. Take swimwear.

The Alonnisos International Marathon was inaugurated in 2005. In 2006 Alonnisos Walking Club participated and created 10 km and 21km walking routes, the objective being not to race but to help participants enjoy a wonderful day's walking. This is the 10 km route. The walk is along established paths and is therefore relatively easy. You will walk through lovely open countryside, olive groves and pine forests to the south west coast, and stop for a swim and lunch at one of the more remote beaches.

With your back to the sea in Patitiri harbour take the right hand road up, past the Alkyon Hotel on the corner. You will pass the National bank on the left and then the post office on the right. A little further on and you will see a big pine tree in the middle of the road in front of you.

Take a look under the last small balcony roof before this on your right. Here you will see the last remaining road sign for the hill you have just climbed, Avenue Ikion Dolopon, or the avenue of the Dolops of Ikos. Ikos was one of the ancient names of Alonnisos, and the Dolops were a race of pirates who were the first known inhabitants here.

Carry on up past the fire station on your left and stop at the crossroads. All around on your left hand side are the small concrete houses that were constructed by the military to re-house the inhabitants of the old village of Alonnisos (Chora in Greek) after the earthquake in 1965, and which effectively created what is now Patitiri.

Take the road around to your left and you will pass the "Ikos" women's co-operative on your left (the spanakopita [spinach pie] and bottled tuna are to die for!) and the junior school on your right. You then come to a T-junction with Technokids directly in front of you. Turn right and then take the road up to the left signposted Chora (old village). Continue on up past the EKO (Esso) petrol station and the road bends sharply to the left outside the entrance to the Atrium hotel on the right. Just outside the Atrium is the privately owned church of Ayios Petros & Ayios Pavlos. Directly in front of you on the opposite side of the hotel drive is a house. To the right of the house is a large concrete wall and a blue sign post reading Mega Nero. Take this footpath up with the concrete wall on your left. You will quickly come to a T-junction where you need to turn right and almost immediately left and go up between a few small outbuildings where there are usually chickens and kids (the goat variety!) being kept. Keep straight ahead and within 20 metres there is a fence straight in front of you. Turn right here along a path with the fence on your left and the pine trees on your right. This leads you out into an old almond grove. The path continues straight along and passes below a very tall new house. As you see this new house above you and to the left, take a small left turn off the main path and go uphill on a short section of concrete to a dirt road, where you turn right and go directly behind the house. Carry on ahead between an old stone wall on your left and a fence on your right. There is sometimes a gate across the path here which you can go through, closing it behind you (see note 1 below if this gate is locked).

Keep to the left and continue on towards a large fig tree, beyond which is a lovely old U-shaped kalivi (a kalivi is a small cottage normally situated in the countryside and used by families to stay in for short periods whilst they are working the olive trees). From the fig tree, cross the almond grove towards the kalivi, past an old grapevine over a metal frame (this is one of the few original Alonnisos grapevines to have survived the outbreak of phylloxera in 1953). You will see a small set of stone steps on the right, at the foot of which on the right is an old amphora set into the ground. Go down the steps and take a look in the "U" of the old kalivi to the left. You will see a set of metal rails on the ground outside a wooden door on the right. Open the door and you will see an old drying rack which used to be pulled out on the rails to dry the grapes in the sun.

With the kalivi on your left there is a lovely view straight ahead to the distinctive triangular peak of Tourkovigla, the 2nd highest point on Alonnisos at 344m. You can walk up Tourkovigla, see "Across the Centre of the Island" walk.

Keeping the kalivi on your left follow the narrow path around it to the left. Below you to the right is the area of "Mega Nero" (big water), and you can see several covered well heads. After a few minutes the path reaches an olive grove and you head slightly right and downhill to the dirt road below, where in front of you will be a large concrete cisterna (water tank)***(this is the point you will re-join the main walk if diverted by the closed gate)*** . With the cisterna in front of you, take the dirt road to the right (ignoring the path downhill to the right which leads to the public spring of Mega Nero). Continue on this dirt road, around a right hand bend and past another road joining from the left and you will come to a T-junction with a wide, surfaced road. Turn left here and almost immediately left again where there is a small fenced-in area of geese, chickens and other assorted wildlife on the right hand side. Walk down this road and take the first dirt road off to the right. You will go past a relatively new house on the left and then a small cement coloured shed-like building also on the left. Electricity poles run the length of this dirt road. Eventually the road ends at a house on the right. Turn left along the path just before the entrance to the house, up the stone steps to the left and enjoy this lovely section through the forest. After a few minutes you will come to some steps down to your left. At the top of the steps to the right is a lovely view across the slate roof of the old church and out to sea. As you go down the steps on the right there are the remains of the stone walls of the old monastery. At the bottom of the steps on the right is the modern church and a little further on the old church of Aghii Anarghiri.

Aghii Anarghiri: the churches of the healing Saints, Agios Kosmas and Agios Damianas. The Saints were 4th century Arab doctors who treated the poor in Athens for no charge - Anarghiri means without payment. The old church dates from the 15th - 16th century and has been carefully restored. Formerly there was a monastery on this site and ruins of the cells can still be seen. The newer church was built just after the second world war. There is a lovely wooden bell tower on the cliff edge and notice the large hole in the ground on the side of the old church nearest to you. This is a cisterna or water tank uncovered during renovation work, as were human remains, believed to be the monks who once lived there. This is a fantastic spot to watch the sunset.

Follow the path along the cliff in front of the old church and down through the forest, with wonderful views of the bay of Megali Amos and its beaches. The path keeps close to the cliff and down to the right of a new house, emerging onto a dirt road. Directly opposite you is a lovely little pebble beach. **This is Tourkoneri beach. The 21 km marathon walk continues from here.** This makes an excellent swim and lunch stop.

From Toukoneri beach, with your back to the sea take the forest road up to the left. This is a fairly long uphill section, so pace yourself!

The old church of Aghii Anarghiri

At the top turn right, past the spring on the left, and simply follow the
road as it winds uphill through the forest (this forest road has many bee
orchids along the edges in spring). You will go through a forest glade with a
small section of low stone wall and a sign to Aghii Anarghiri on your right.
Keep straight on past a new house on your right, until you come to a T
junction with a stone wall facing you. Turn right here, follow the road and,
after some time and having passed many established cypress trees on
your left, the road will bend sharply to the left. This area is called Raches
or spine. Walk around the bend and as you go downhill you will see below you
in the forest to the right the remains of a ramshackle goat encampment.
Follow the road down and around to the right at the bottom and just
around the corner you will see a large number of cylindrical metal
containers. This is the collection point for the resin tapped from the pine
trees. Take a look and you will see how it changes from a clear sticky liquid
into a hard white wax-like substance.

Resin collection used to be a thriving business on the island: in the 1950's there were 20 resin collectors on Alonnisos but now there is only one (if you see him his name is Stelios). If you are walking through the forest and you suddenly find that your path stops abruptly, it is probable that you have found one of the old resin trails. Most of the pine trees on Alonnisos are Aleppo pines. Resin collection is very hard work: a strip of bark is peeled from the trunk of the tree and a collection tin (in other parts of Greece plastic sacks are used instead) is hammered into the tree below the scar. Acid is applied to the top of the scar to encourage the tree to 'bleed'. When the collection tin is full the contents are tipped into large barrels and left to harden. Be warned: the resin is incredibly sticky and takes an age to get off. At one time the resin was sent to Halkida on Evia but now it goes to Athens. After processing it yields turpentine, rosin for stringed instruments, and compounds used in paints, medicines, cleaning and household products, disinfectants and varnishes. Of course, it is also used to give the flavouring for retsina. The tradition of resinating wine is believed to have derived from the practice of sealing amphorae with the waxy resin to avoid deterioration in transit: the flavour then leached into the wine itself and the result became an acquired taste. I have also heard it said that a lump of the hardened resin was put into wine when carried in animal skins to act as a preservative. Another story has it that the flavour was added deliberately to discourage the Turks from stealing the stuff! Most retsina is produced in the Attica region of Greece and, rather surprisingly, its largest market outside of domestic consumption is the UK.

Continue on the same road past this point, ignoring the left turn to the main asphalt road behind the builder's yard. You will pass the entrance to the International Academy of Classical Homeopathy on your left (if you have an interest in homeopathy you may visit to make enquiries), then on your right the geese, etc. which you passed earlier. Follow the road around to the left until it meets the main asphalt road. Turn right and follow the road past the turning on the left to Votsi and back into Patitiri.

*Note 1: if for some reason it is not possible to get through this new gate then just follow the main path through the old almond grove you were on before and continue straight ahead below the new house. The path turns right and downhill past another house on the left. Follow the path around to the left and under this second house (do not go straight down!). The path continues left around the hillside until it drops down to the right and you come out with the spring of Mega Nero on your left. With the spring at your back take the left path uphill for a few minutes and you will arrive at the concrete cisterna mentioned above**

The 21km Marathon Walk

Main Route: *Patitiri - Mega Nero - Aghii Anarghiri - Tourkoneri Beach - Megali Amos Bay & Beach - Kastraki Archaeological Site - Raches Pine Resin Collection Point - Patitiri*

Distance: 21 kms

Time 7-8 hours without stops

Swim Stop: Yes at Tourkoneri & Megali Amos

No Tavernas

Walking shoes/boots recommended. Shorts are ok. Take swimwear.

Follow the 10 km marathon walk to Toukoneri beach.

Refer to the map for the 10km Marathon Walk on page 26.

From Toukoneri beach, with your back to the sea take the forest road up to the left. This is a fairly long uphill section, pace yourself. At the top of the hill you come to a T junction with a dirt road. At the very top of the hill on the left look for a red spot marker. You will see that this marks the beginning of a forest trail which heads down to the left. Follow this trail until it emerges onto a gravel road (if you turn left at the top of the hill onto the dirt road you will come to the same point).

Turn left and downhill on the gravel road, at the bottom go through the green gate on the left (closing it behind you). Take the path down and keep to the right, following the path which goes slightly uphill (if you follow this path straight down you will come to the next small pebble beach around the bay fromTourkoneri). Follow this path along the cliff and you will soon begin to descend and see a house below you and to the left. The path emerges onto a dirt road, turn left and you will be facing the gate across the driveway to this house. On your right you will see a small path heading down towards the sea. Follow it down towards the sea where it turns right along the coast (to your left is a small concrete slipway and an old boat house). After about 100m the path turns to the left and drops down one terrace level over a stone wall. At this point on the left is the way down to a small shingle beach, a perfect place for another swim stop.

When you leave the beach turn to the left and follow the path up and to the right.

Although not part of the marathon route, there is a small diversion from here which will take you to the main pebble beach of Megali Amos bay. When you leave the small shingle beach turn to the left and follow the coastal path past a ruined kalivi on your right, through a stand of large pine trees, then follow the path close to the coast and to the left of a stone wall below a big house. The beach is down to your left. When you leave return the same way but just before the stand of pine trees turn sharply uphill to your left across the terraces. The big house is on your left and you will come out opposite the driveway to a small stone cottage on the dirt road a short distance up from the shrine*.

You will quickly emerge at the end of a dirt road marked by a small shrine*. Turn left and follow this road up until you come to a T junction with a wider gravel road. Here you turn to the right and follow the road uphill until you come to the next junction where a road joins from the left. Turn left here and follow this road until on a bend on your right hand side you see a trekking map and waymarker for path number 8 to Meghalo Chorafi. Follow this path up and after about 10 minutes you will come to a rough gate which you simply go through and re-tie behind you. Then after about another 10 minutes keep a lookout for a red spot marker on a large stone in the middle of the path, across which there is a fallen pine tree. This marks where there is a path leading off to the right. Take this path off to the right and follow it up until it emerges at the end of a rough dirt track.

On your right hand side is the archaeological site of Kastraki, an ancient hill-top fortified look-out point guarding the northern approach to Alonnisos. Neolithic tools have been discovered here. Just after you meet the track there is a reasonably flat olive grove on your right. This makes for a shady rest stop and a chance to explore Kastraki if you wish. If you do wish to explore then as you turn right into the olive grove, with the hill of Kastraki on your right, walk along the edge of the hill until you see the most obvious goat track going up and follow it to the top. The views and tranquility there are worth the climb.

Leaving Kastraki behind follow the track up to where another track joins from the left. Keep heading right and you will soon come to a T junction with a dirt road where there is a new house on the right hand corner. The view down to Kokkinokastro and the islet of Kokkinonisi (also locally known as Vrachos) from here is wonderful.

Kokkinokastro is believed to be the site of ancient Ikos. The cemetery discovered there dates from the mesolithic period. According to legend one of the graves (mnimata) is said to be that of King Peleus, the father of Achilles. Paleolithic remains have been discovered on the nearby islet of Vrachos.

Turn right here and follow the road down, ignoring any side turnings, until you come to a T junction with a main dirt road. Turn left here and follow the road along until you come to a point where there is a stone wall on your left and a turning off to the right sign posted to Aghii Anargiri. Follow the road straight ahead and after some time, having passed many established cypress trees on your left, the road will bend sharply to the left. This area is called Raches or spine. Walk around the bend and as you go downhill you will see below you in the forest to the right the remains of a ramshackle goat encampment. Follow the road down and around to the right at the bottom and just around the corner on the right you will see a large number of cylindrical metal containers. This is the collection point for the resin tapped from the pine trees. Take a look and you will see how it changes from a clear sticky liquid into a hard white wax-like substance (see highlighted text in 10 km marathon walk).

Continue on the same road past this point, ignoring the left turn to the asphalt road behind the builder's yard. You will pass the entrance to the International Academy of Classical Homeopathy on your left (if you have an interest in homeopathy you may visit to make enquiries), then on the right the geese etc which you passed earlier. Follow the road around to the left until it meets the main asphalt road. Turn right and follow the road past the turning on the left to Votsi and back into Patitiri.

Near the road from Lefto Yialos to Tzortzi Yialos

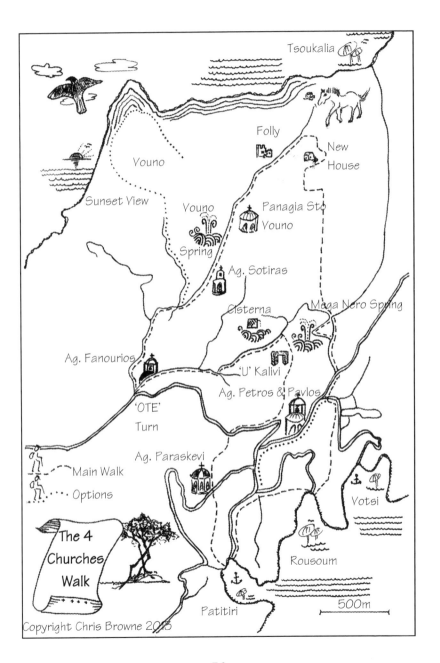

Tsoukalia

Folly

New House

Vouno

Panagia Sto Vouno

Sunset View

Vouno

Spring

Ag. Sotiras

Cisterna

Mega Nero Spring

Ag. Fanourios

'U' Kalivi

Ag. Petros & Pavlos

'OTE' Turn

Ag. Paraskevi

Main Walk

Options

Votsi

The 4 Churches Walk

Rousoum

Patitiri

500m

Copyright Chris Browne 2015

38

The 4 Churches Walk

Main Route: *Patitiri - Ayia Paraskevi - Ayios Fanourios - Ayios Sotiras - Vouno Spring - Panagia sto Vouno - Mega Nero - Rousoum Beach - Patitiri*

Includes an optional circuit around the hill of Vouno.

This walk can be started from the Old Village. Walk down the asphalt road towards Patitiri and join the walk at the "OTE" turn described below.

Distance: 10 kms

Time: 3-4 hours without stops

Swim Stop: Yes

Taverna: Yes at Rousoum beach

Walking shoes recommended. Shorts ok. Take swimwear.

You start by walking through the back streets above Patitiri; like all Greek villages this will seem like a bit of a maze. If you feel you are lost, or if a path is blocked, simply ask for the church of Ayia Paraskevi. The walk then takes you through the open countryside and hills above Patitiri to the lovely old church of Panagia sto Vouno, from where there are wonderful views. The route then continues along one of the nicest forest trails on the island, past the allotments of Mega Nero, to the "locals" beach at Rousoum and then back to Patitiri. The walk is mostly along main footpaths and dirt roads. The optional circuit around the hill of Vouno is short and recommended for the views and the poppies in spring.

With your back to the sea in Patitiri take the road to the left, away from the harbour. After just a few metres on your right there is a bakery. Turn right into the alleyway immediately before the bakery. Follow this path around to the left, then to the right and up the steps in front of you.

These lead you up to the entrance of the Pleiades Pension. With the gate to the Pleiades on your right walk up a concrete path, across a small road and up another steep concrete path. At the top of this you will meet a paved road where you turn left and continue to walk uphill. Keep following the paved road until it divides and take the left-hand fork. Follow this road but beware the steep drop to the left. At the end of this road there is a sharp turn to the right followed by a sharp turn to the left. When you get to the end of this road you will meet the main asphalt road and the church of Ayia Paraskevi is directly opposite.

It is ok to take a look inside the church if you wish, provided you are appropriately dressed. This is the church used for most weddings and funerals, the smaller churches in the countryside being used on their particular Saint's day.

To the right of the church is Kaloyianni's hardware emporium, a must see for DIY enthusiasts! Take the small road between the church and the hardware shop and continue straight on until you meet a garden wall in front of you. Turn right here and continue until you come to a junction where you keep left. The road now starts climbing; on the right look for a "Leader" board outside Kostas' carpentry workshop. Above you to the left is a very unattractive large off-white concrete building, this is the defunct open-air cinema.

Continue on up this road until you join the asphalt road. Turn right here and walk down the road. There are houses on both sides of the road and after a few minutes on the right there will be a white house with a stone garden wall, a fig tree and oleander outside, and a black wrought iron sign reading "Dio Adelphi Spiti". Just before this house on your left is a small path going up into an olive and almond grove. Take this path and follow it along with a stone terrace wall on your left until you pass behind a house on the right between you and the road. Just below this house on the bend in the main road is the Atrium hotel and the new church of Ayios Petros & Ayios Pavlos, privately owned by the Vafinis family, owners of the Atrium hotel (if you wish to visit this church simply turn down to the right immediately after the house and return the same way). Continue straight on and after a few metres turn left and go up between a few small outbuildings where there are usually chickens and kids (the goat variety!) being kept. Keep straight ahead and

"Lamentation at the tomb"

within 20 metres there is a fence straight in front of you. Turn right here along a path with the fence on your left and pine trees on your right. This leads you out into an old almond grove. Along this section there are lovely views over the fishing village of Votsi and out to sea. The path continues straight along and passes below a very tall new house. As you see this new house above you and to the left, take a small left turn off the main path and go uphill to a dirt road, where you turn right and go directly behind the house. Carry on ahead between an old stone wall on your left and a fence on your right. There is sometimes a gate across the path here which you can go through, closing it behind you **(see note 1 below if this gate is locked)**.

Keep to the left and continue on towards a large fig tree, beyond which is a lovely old U-shaped kalivi (a small cottage normally situated in the countryside and used by families to stay in for short periods whilst they are working the olive trees). From the fig tree, cross the almond grove towards the kalivi, past an old grapevine over a metal frame (this is one of

41

the few original Alonnisos grapevines to have survived the outbreak of phylloxera in 1953). You will see a small set of stone steps on the right, at the foot of which on the right is an old amphora set into the ground. Go down the steps and take a look in the "U" of the old kalivi to the left. You will see a set of metal rails on the ground outside an old wooden door on the right. Open the door and you will see a drying rack which used to be pulled out on the rails to dry the grapes in the sun.

With the kalivi on your left there is a lovely view straight ahead to the distinctive triangular peak of Tourkovigla, the 2nd highest point on Alonnisos at 344m. You can walk up Tourkovigla, see the "Across the Centre of the Island" walk.

Keeping the kalivi on your left follow the narrow path around it to the left. Below you to the right is the area of "Mega Nero" (big water), and you can see several covered well-heads. After a few minutes the path reaches an olive grove and you head slightly right and downhill to the dirt road below, where in front of you will be a large concrete cisterna (water tank) * *(this is the point you will re-join the main walk if diverted by the closed gate)* .

With the cisterna in front of you, take the dirt road to the left which goes uphill past many small-holdings. At the top is a vineyard on your left and a junction at which you turn right. Continue along this road which has great views over Patitiri to your left and, after a few minutes, up to the Old Village in front of you. You will emerge at a sharp bend on the asphalt road (locally known as the "OTE" turn, OTE being the tele-comms company - their antenna towers are at the top of this hill).

Turn right here and cross to the opposite side of the road to enjoy the view down to Yalia beach and the restored windmill. Above you to the right is the "Sunset Café" and the private church of Ayios Fanourios is located in the grounds. If you wish to visit the church the turning is a little way further on your right and well worth a few minutes for the view you get out over both sides of the island and up to the old village. Continue on up this road to a junction and take the right fork onto a dirt road (the left goes to the landfill site!).

After a few minutes you will come to two turns on the right close together, take the second and most obvious of these. **Immediately on your right is "kitty city" the ASAP main cat refuge on the island and worth a visit in itself!** Continue along this road and you will soon pass the church of Ayios Sotiras nestling in a stand of tall cypress trees just below the road to the right down a short concrete ramp.

Return to the road, turn right and continue on past a few houses on the right. The road now starts to descend. As you look straight ahead and slightly to the right you will see the lovely church of Panagia sto Vouno (Mary of the mountain) with a new and incredibly ugly concrete cisterna to its right. Carry on down and at the bottom of the hill on your left is the spring of Vouno (Vouno being the name of this area and meaning hill or mountain).

This spring is probably the most favoured collection point for drinking water and according to legend the water from it comes undersea from the Pelion. This was proven to be true in recent years by a geological survey of underground water reserves on the island.

A little way past the spring on the right as the road begins to climb again is the path to the church. Unfortunately this church is normally locked.

Church of the Panaghia at Vouno: this is a basilica with a cupola, dating from the 16th - 17th century. The church had marvellous frescoes depicting Christ and His apostles until some over-enthusiastic spring cleaning covered them with a layer of asvesti (whitewash). The celebrations at this church take place on the 23rd August to mark the birth of the Virgin.

The church of Panagia sto Vouno

Continue on up the road and as the road levels out at the top you will go past the "folly" on the left, a stone cottage with a strange tower built on the right side, inspired by a visit to Windsor castle by the owner! A little further on to your left where you can see an electricity pole heading up into the olive trees you can just see a small building on the top of the ridge. This is the seismological station which records all the earth tremors.

This area is home to a large conspiracy of ravens (yes I had to look it up!) and is also a fantastic place to spot Eleonora's falcons and bee-eaters. Carry on as the road now starts to gently go downhill and keep a sharp lookout for the roof of a new house at the bottom of the olive grove on your right. Just ahead of you at this point is an overgrown rough road which joins on the right and immediately before this you need to head straight down through the olive grove on your right (there is usually an old

44

Landrover ahead of you on the left at this point). There are many carob trees around here. Walk more or less straight down through the olive grove to the house, turn right down the road and around to the left at the bottom: the church of Panagia sto Vouno is now above you to the right.

Continue on this forest road and ignore turnings to the left and right. Beyond this turn you will pass a fenced area on the left normally full of turkeys and other assorted birds. You will come out at a T junction with another dirt road, turn left and almost immediately turn right at the next T junction.

To visit the public spring of Mega Nero take the next right turn. The spring is about 200m down this track and you can then take the path on the left as you look at the spring to re-join the road you were on. You then turn right to join the main asphalt road.

Follow this road as it bends around to the left and joins the main asphalt road along the island. Turn right here and follow the road as it goes around an S bend, first left then right and meets another road joining from the left (there is a traffic mirror on the corner).

If you wish to go directly back to Patitiri from here simply keep on the road straight ahead.

Take this left turn towards Votsi and opposite the second mini-market on the left there is a road going off to the right, just before Aneza's hairdressing salon. Follow this road to the end and turn right. You will quickly come to a large open area on your left where you turn left and follow the road in and around to the right as it turns into a path and then stone steps which lead you down between some houses to Rousoum beach.

You can walk out onto Rousoum headland from here. With the beach on your right look back the way you came and go up the steps in front of you. After just a few steps turn right, go up a few more steps and then follow the path along the coast, past a house and a low stone wall. At the end of the path you will come to a small shed, take the path to the right to go down onto the rocks. Return the same way.

Walk along the back of the beach past a few tavernas and up the stone steps at the far end. Follow the steps up, across a concrete road, and up again past the Gorgona hotel on your left. At the top of the steps turn left on the concrete road, left again at the top, and you will be at the top of the main hill from Patitiri harbour close to the council offices and medical centre.

Note 1: If for some reason it is not possible to get through the gate then just follow the main path through the old almond grove you were on before and go straight on below the new house. The path turns right and downhill past a house on the left, keep left under the house (don't go straight on down!) and the path continues left around the hillside until it drops down to the right and you come to the spring at Mega Nero on your left. With the spring at your back take the left path uphill for a few minutes and you will arrive at the concrete cisterna mentioned above*.

Optional circuit around the hill of Vouno:

Continue on up this road and ignore any side turnings. When you reach the top the road bears sharply to the left where a big pine tree is on the corner and the fenced in area for the OTE towers is opposite you to the left. Follow the road up and round to the left and again keep to the left at the gates to the OTE compound. Follow this dirt road down and through a short section of pine forest. As you leave the forest line there are olive groves on both left and right*(you will **return through the olive grove on your right**) and fabulous views on the left across to Skopelos and the Pelion. Continue along this road with the sea on your left past Kates polytunnel and "shed" (anywhere along here is a fabulous place to watch the sunset and on a clear day looking directly out to sea from anywhere near the "shed" mount Olympus is straight ahead and mount Athos off to your right just beyond the edge of Alonnisos). At the end of the road there is a big pine tree and an old ruined stone shelter off to your left, a wonderful place to enjoy the views over the bay of Megali Amos and across to the islets of Stavros then Manolas. Below the big pine tree and to the right you will find a path that leads into the forest. Follow this short path through the forest until you emerge in a roughly circular field sloping sharply down from right to left. In spring and early summer this field is usually carpeted with poppies. Return the way you came and turn left through the olive grove mentioned previously*. Follow the track going down and slightly to the right through the olive grove, past lots of wild oregano, and you emerge back at the big pine tree on the corner next to the OTE compound. Take the road downhill and back to *"kitty city"* and the main route.

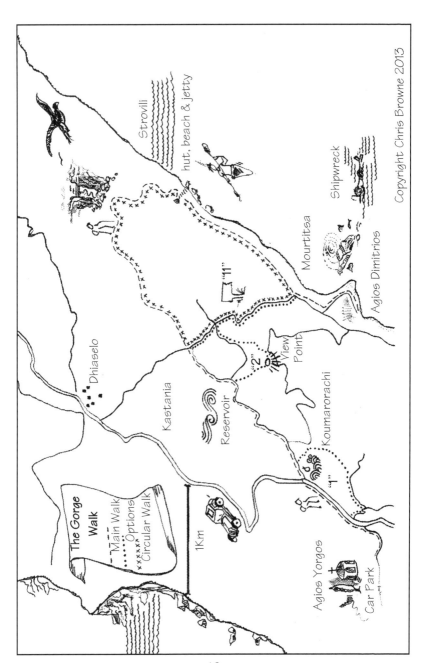

The Gorge Walk

- - - Main Walk
······ Options
××××× Circular Walk

Strovili

hut, beach & jetty

Shipwreck

Mourtitsa

Agios Dimitrios

"11"

Dhiaselo

Kastania

Reservoir

"2"

View Point

Koumarorachi

"4"

1Km

Agios Yorgos

Car Park

Copyright Chris Browne 2013

48

The Gorge Walk

Main Route: *Ayios Yorgos Church - Kastania Gorge - Strovili Beach – Mourtitsa - Ayios Dimitrios Beach*

Shorter Circular route option

2 Optional variations

Distance: 12 kms (the gorge itself is 4kms)

Time: 4-5 hours without stops

Footwear: Due to the terrain, boots or sturdy walking shoes are essential. If you intend doing the walk as a circular route up or down footpath number 11 then long trousers or zip-on "legs" are recommended.

Swim stop: Yes

Kantina: Yes at Ayios Dimitrios (June to September)

*A **new reservoir has been constructed in this area and starting from Dhiaselo is no longer possible due to construction work.***

This walk should present no problem to walkers of reasonable fitness but does involve a fair amount of clambering over boulders in the gorge. The start point is at around 300m elevation down to sea level so it is nearly all downhill.

This walk is totally different from anything else on Alonnisos and you will walk through countryside covered with strawberry trees, Judas trees, tree heather, Montpelier Maple and wonderful olive groves. Along the way you may see Eleonora's falcons (particularly near the area of surface water described later when you start from Ayios Yorgos). Where the gorge meets the sea at Strovili, a pair of Bonelli's eagles nest in the cliffs every year. You will need to organise transport to get you to and from the north of the island.

The walk finishes at the lovely pebble beach of Ayios Dimitrios. You can also make the walk as a shorter circular route if you wish, either by starting at Kastania or at Mourtitsa on the coast. Taxi drivers are reliable and if you take a taxi to your chosen start point just ask the driver to pick you up from where you intend finishing at a certain time and, give or take the odd half hour, he'll be there! Taxis will not drive on rough roads though. Since discovering this route in 1997 I have always led this walk from the start point of the little church of Ayios Yorgos as it's my favourite route, so this is the one described.

To get to the start point:

Head north along the island to where the road divides with Steni Vala to the right and Gerakas up to the left. Take the road to Gerakas and after 4.5 km you will see a small side turn going up on your left to the car park area at the church of Ayios Yorgos. This is at one end of path number 12.

At Ayios Yorgos: Before you start walking, stand in the circular car parking area to take in the fabulous view to the islands of the Marine Park.

The nearest island is **Peristera** (dove), beyond and slightly to the right are the two islands of **Dio Adelphi** (Two Brothers), the beautiful island of **Skantzoura** with its unique coastline of white marbelised limestone and juniper forests, and beyond them both on the horizon is **Skyros**, around 35 miles from where you stand and easily visible on a clear day. Way off to the right on a clear day you will see the northern end of **Evia**, with its high point of Mount Dirfus. Looking north to your left the nearest island is **Kyra Panagia**, rising up beyond is **Gioura** with the cave of Cyclops and off in the distance and slightly to the right is **Piperi**, the core zone of the marine park.

You may also like to take a look inside the little church just below the car parking area before you set off, just remember to close the gate! The BBC recorded a TV programme here with Ainsley Harriot in 1997. There is also a small spring to the right of the church gate. See optional variation 1

Walk left on the tarmac road and after about 10 minutes on your right you will see a new building (a pumping station for the new reservoir) and below it a small area of surface water surrounded by a bank of grey shale. Go past the turning to this new building, around the bend and immediately turn right at the signpost reading Koumarorachi (**Κουμαρόραχη**), Gerakas (**Γέρακας**), and Dhiaselo (**Διάσελο**) are straight ahead on the tarmac road. There is also a large notice board for the reservoir project now. Continue past the water, where you may see Eleonora's falcons hunting insects. Continue along this road, ignoring the dirt road going off on the right. You will pass a corrugated iron goat pen with a concrete water cisterna on the right of a left hand bend and then you will come to a junction where a smaller road goes up to the right. Ignore this turning and keep to the main road downhill with the new reservoir below you to the left.

Circular Route option start/finish point. See below

See optional variation 2 Continue down this road and on the right of a left hand bend you will see a track going up to the right with a handpainted sign reading "Ayios Dimitrios". This is waymarked footpath number 11. On your left is a large concrete construction.

Keep to the road which now goes sharply downhill, and take the small path which goes straight on and slightly to the right at the bottom. On your left is a new building and the beginning of the river bed. On your right is a small kalivi (cottage). Continue on the path which is marked by red spots for a few hundred metres and then follow the markers down to the left and into the river bed.

Now take your time and simply follow the gorge down to the sea. Along the way in early spring/summer you will see lots of small mauve campanula along the walls of the gorge and many hollyoak trees. Some of the best views will be behind you as you go farther down and the walls of the gorge become ever steeper, so it's worth stopping every now and again to soak up the silence and the views. You will pass several places where the goats and the rain have brought down a run of stones into

Bellflowers (*Campanula*) in Kastania gorge

the bottom of the gorge, and you may come across the odd goat carcass or skeleton. At one point just before the gorge turns into a really narrow short section there is a high reddish coloured curved area above you to the left. In September just this one area is covered in beautiful yellow sternbergea flowers. About half way down and on the right you will see two small raised terraces, the second larger than the first, built up from the natural rock formations. There is a large stone cairn on the second terrace.

These are the places where in years gone by trees that were cut on the hills above were turned into charcoal for use by the shepherds. Local folklore has it that in history marauding pirates who systematically foraged further and further up the gorge, were the ones who established the settlement of Dhiaselo mentioned earlier.

Sadly there is now quite a lot of disused building materials washed down into the gorge from the new reservoir. Eventually you will make the last right turn and see the sea again and very soon on your left you will see an olive tree growing almost horizontally and providing some welcome shade. If you do stop here it is on the cliffs behind you that the Bonelli's eagles nest every year. Continue on down towards the sea at Strovili and take the marked right turn a few hundred metres before the sea and up into a small olive grove from where there is a good view back along the river bed you have walked down, and also across to the northern end of Peristera island. As you look at the sea and Peristera there is an obvious trail from the olive grove to the right which runs parallel to the sea. Follow this trail and after a couple of minutes you will arrive at a wall of vegetation. The trail enters immediately to the left of a large strawberry tree. Follow the trail in and very shortly you will come out at the corner of a fence line on your left. The fence has a large hole in it. Go through the hole and if you fancy a swim go straight down to the little wooden shack below you, down the steps and onto the little beach on the left or dive straight off the tumbledown jetty! This a great picnic spot and if you swim north from the jetty for about 20m you will find a lovely little cave with a small beach inside, typical of the sort of place that monk seals favour.

From here look across to the northern half of Peristera and you will see a short vertical section of bare earth. This is the only visible entrance to one of several old iron and chromite mines.

When you leave here you need to cross this fenced area parallel to the sea about halfway up between the coast and the upper fence line you entered through. You will see a hole in the fence on the opposite side. Go through this hole and follow the goat track, keeping more or less parallel to the sea (if in doubt when faced with a series of goat paths here...keep low!).

Take a moment along this section to look down to the beds of Poseidonia (sea weed) in the sea below. These appear as black patches in an otherwise turquoise sea. Poseidonia is a protected species which oxygenates the sea, stabilises the sea bed, and provides a habitat for marine life. This is one of the reasons why the sea is so clear around Alonnisos. The small fluffy brown balls you find on beaches, particularly Chrisi Milia and Ayios Dimitrios, are bits of this plant.

After about 15 minutes you will come to the end of the goat track and descend onto one end of a rough dirt road. Turn right and follow this road past a line of rocks across the road and through a gate. Continue on this road.

Circular Route option mid point. See below

To your left are the very pretty pebble beaches of Mourtitsa. Simply carry on this road past a very large new house on the left and, where the dirt road meets the tarmac, there is a rough road down to the left signed to Ayios Dimitrios beach. Take this road down to the left. There are the remains of a Byzantine basilica to your right and at the back of the beach a small sunken field which is flooded with rain water over the winter months and attracts many migrating birds in spring and late summer. In high season there is a Kantina open behind the middle of the beach and at the far end, next to the small jetty, Yiannis little taverna normally run by his daughter Magda. A great place to chill out and congratulate yourselves with a cold beer, after a refreshing swim of course!

Taxis will normally drive down to meet you at the Kantina. To give you some idea of time, the walks I led down the gorge left Patitiri at 0900 to get to the start point of Ayios Yorgos. We usually reached Strovili around 1400 and got picked up from Ayios Dimitrios at 1700.

Circular Route Option start/finish point. If you wish to walk the gorge as a shorter circular route then this is one possible start point. From here you can go down the gorge, along the coast to Mourtitsa and then return on path number 11. Or you can go up path number 11 and down to Mourtitsa, then along the coast and return up the gorge. You can also drive to Mourtitsa on the coast and start and finish there if you wish.

Circular walk Option mid point. If you are doing the walk as a circular route, keep a sharp lookout on your right for the waymarker to footpath number 11. The earth bank to the right is quite steep and the path starts by going up and over some water pipes at ground level and is just before a distinctive new house on the left hand side which is on several levels. Footpath 11 from here is a steep climb and when you reach the top you will come to a dirt road, which you go more or less straight across and down footpath 11.

Optional Variation 1

Turn left on the tarmac road and almost immediately on your right is a rough dirt track. Turn onto this track and follow it down, ignoring all side turns (as you take this right turn there are usually beehives behind the bushes to your left). As you walk down and look out to sea you will see a small hill off to your right with a stone ruin near the top. When you reach a level area at the bottom there will be an olive grove on your left and the hill with the stone ruin in front of you to the right. The track you are on continues straight ahead to the left of this hill. Turn left into the olive grove and continue along the small path and slightly downhill. At the end of the olive grove you need to walk up the terraces straight in front you and, at the top between some bushes, you will find the path continues up and around to the left, then bends to the right and straightens out until you come out to the right hand side of the surface water. Turn right on the road past the water and re-join the main route.

Optional Variation 2

The road up to the right immediately turns left and eventually bisects path 11 and stops at a small collection of shepherds' cottages. On the right hand side of this first left bend there is a reasonably clear hillside covered in thyme going up to your right. Walk straight up this hill for just a couple of minutes and you will see a goat track going left where there are usually many sea squills. Go left up over a low terrace wall and then immediately right and uphill again. Go past the first small track on the right and take the next and higher track in to the right between low bushes. This will lead you to a wonderful flat viewpoint with Peristera directly opposite and the beach of Ayios Dimitrios below you slightly to the right. Looking out to sea go right then immediately down to the left and follow the track to where it meets the continuation of the dirt road you were on earlier. Bear right along this road and you will come to path number 11 on either side. Take the path down to the left and you will come out back on the approach road to the gorge, where you turn right.

The Old Village and Beyond

Main Route: *Patitiri - Old Village (via the Old Donkey Track) - Kalovoulos Peak - Cape Kokkino - Mikros Mourtias beach - Old Village*

Alternative start point from the bus stop in the Old Village

Includes optional walk from the Old Village to the beaches of Vrisitsa and Yalia plus a short diversion through the Old Village itself.

Main Route Distance: 10 kms

Time: 4-5 hours without stops

Swim stop: Yes at Mikros Mourtias

Taverna: In Old Village

Walking shoes or boots recommended. Make sure you have long trousers with you. Take swimwear.

This walk takes you to the Old Village via the traditional cobbled footpath. The main walk and optional walk can also be started from the Old Village. As a small diversion you can explore the Old Village. The main walk then continues through open countryside to Kalovoulos peak, down to the coast and back to the Old Village (you can omit the walk up and down Kalovoulos if you wish). A lot of the route is rough underfoot and involves several hills plus one steep descent towards Cape Kokkino. It is therefore quite taxing.

With your back to the sea in Patitiri take the left hand road away from the harbour. Ignore the first road on the left and carry on past shops and supermarkets on your left and a petrol station on your right. Continue on the road and after about 500m on your left you see a small concrete road with one of the large trekking maps mounted there. Turn left here onto path number 4. This is the beginning of the "old donkey track", a lovely old

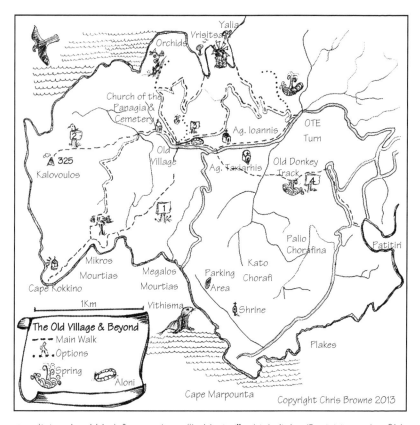

The Old Village & Beyond

- - - Main Walk
...🚶 Options
🌊 Spring

1Km

Copyright Chris Browne 2013

traditional cobbled footpath or "kalderimi" which links Patitiri to the Old Village. Continue up this footpath, the edges of which are a great place to spot orchids and herbs in the spring and Myrtle trees at anytime, until you come to a T-junction with a public cisterna (water tank) in front of you. Turn right here and continue on up until you reach a dirt road.

There is a wonderful view of the Old Village from here with the Kastro (castle) at the top. Beyond is the peak of Kalovoulos, the 3rd highest point on Alonnisos at 325m, which is one of your destinations on this walk.

Go straight across the dirt road and continue on the paved donkey track until you meet the asphalt road.

Turn left here and follow the road up, past the aloni on your right, until you come to the main entrance to the Old Village at the top of the hill on your left. The bus stop is here. **This is an alternative start point.**

A short walk through the Old Village: with the bus stop on your right walk up the road to the platela (square) at the top. On your left is the 17th century Church of Christ. Follow the steps up to the left around the back of the church, the door into the church is usually open (it is unusual in that is has a gallery for women to worship). You will come to a small terrace with a café and a great view. On your right take the path up and past the memorial to 9 islanders who were shot by the Nazis on the 15th August 1944 during the festival of Panagia. Just past this memorial is a small museum depicting a traditional village house. Continue ahead past the old doorway and outer wall of the Kastro on your right (you can explore up and down on both sides of this path), past the Paraport Taverna and onto the end for the view. Return to the bus stop .

Continue past the entrance to the Old Village and you soon come to the little church of Panagia and the one cemetery on the island, which is very pretty at night with all the oil lamps lit.

This church of the Panagia is used for the service to mark the Assumption of the Virgin Mary on August 15th.

Keep left past the church and, just before a turning to Mikros Mourtias on your left, on your right you will see the paved start of path number 2. This route will take you up to the summit of Kalovoulos, the 3rd highest point on Alonnisos at 325m. With time to take in the views from the top, up and down will take about 1 hour 30 minutes. During the walk up it is worth stopping from time to time to enjoy the ever-changing views back to the Old Village and beyond. There is one point on the way up where there is a "junction" in the path, keep to the right and uphill. When you reach the top there is a small stone goat pen on the right. Take a few steps to the left here for the view down to the Old Village, Megalos Mourtias beach and along the coast both sides of Alonnisos. If you want to get to the very top turn right at the goat pen and follow the rough path up. After about 10 minutes you arrive at the trig point marking the summit. Return to the bottom, turn right and follow the road around the base of Kalovoulos *(if you prefer an easier route down to the beach turn left here and then right onto the dirt road down to Mikros Mourtias).* After about 15 minutes you will pass a road up on the right to a solitary house and then the road divides and you keep to the left and down into an olive grove. From here the path winds down and across the hillside towards your destination, which is the coast.

This can be quite a difficult path to find at times as it criss-crosses the olive groves on the way down but the route is where the stone walls are at their lowest. You should aim straight for the coast and be down this section in about 15/20 minutes.

When you have a clear view to the sea look for a single large pine tree below you and head slightly to the right of this and you will join a coastal footpath. Turn right to visit the small solar lighthouse at Cape Kokkino on the very southern tip of Alonnisos.

This path soon becomes a rocky goat track which you simply follow along the coast. There is one gate for the goats which you should close behind you. Cape Kokkino is a favourite place for locals to go fishing as the surrounding waters are very deep. On your return continue on the path past the point where you joined from above earlier and you will come to the beach of Mikros Mourtias. From here you take the path up from the back of the beach to join the road. As you start to walk up the road there is a marker for path number 1 on the right. Follow this up to the Old Village and the first building you come to on the right is the old school building.

From here continue on up the paved footpath and take the first right turn, or continue farther up the path until you come to a T-junction with another path with a building in front of you, then turn right. Simply follow either of these routes as they wind between the houses and out to the main street of the Old Village by the bus stop.

That's probably enough walking for one day! If so then perhaps you would like to relax with a drink under the trees opposite taverna Panselinos by the bus stop. If you walk across the road from the bus stop you can look down on the south west coast and the following walk to **The Beaches of Vrisitsa & Yalia** for another day.

Some of the many steps and balconies in the Old Village

The Beaches of Vrisitsa & Yalia

This walk will take you about 2.5 - 3 hours. Both beaches suffer from wind blown debris at times but the views along the way are lovely.

From the bus stop in the Old Village turn right down the asphalt road and just before the aloni on your left there is a turning on the left onto a dirt road. Take this turn and the road immediately divides into 2. Take the left turn and follow the road as it winds around and down below the Old Village towards the small beach of Vrisitsa (the right turn takes you directly to the beach of Yalia).

> Note: at the time of writing, waymarked walking path number 3 has just been cleared and is now usable again. It leads down to Vrisitsa beach from the Alonia (threshing circles). Take the left turn onto the dirt road mentioned above and immediately turn right towards Yalia. On your right is a new house with a black metal gate across a driveway: exactly opposite this on the left you will see the path going downhill. Near the bottom you will see a lovely old capped spring on the left in the trees. You may like to walk back up this path from the beach instead of returning on the dirt road.

After about 30 minutes along this road look for a small path going into the undergrowth on the left at a small passing place, just before a right hand bend (the path is usually marked by a red arrow on a stone). This leads up to a bare looking olive grove on the hill in front of you when looking out to sea. This hillside is a great place for orchids in early spring.

To walk out onto this hillside follow the path up from the passing place, through the heather and go through the usual rebar gate in the goat fence, securing it behind you. Head downhill to your right and follow the obvious path across to the lovely old terraces. The path will quickly take you past some large ruined stone walls on your left, marked by red paint spots. From here is a good place to explore the hillside up to the peak on your left. The views from the top to the Old Village and along the west coast to the north are stunning. In this direction you will also see the bottom of the landfill site. Rubbish has to go somewhere but you will sadly still see some of it falling down the hillside into the seas of the marine park. Continue down the road, past a new house on the left, to the beach.

Re-trace your steps to the start point and take the right hand turn towards Yalia and you will then follow the road down and come to a T-junction on a bend with another dirt road. Turn left here and down to Yalia beach, where there is a very pretty restored windmill, a poignant sign on the side of an old boat and a large water pumping station behind the beach (most of Patitiri's water comes from here). To return you can either go back the way you came or ignore the right hand turn you came down and continue straight on up the road.

Near the top on a sharp right hand bend there is a road leading off to the left. Although this is a dead end it is a nice walk and goes past a defunct spring along the way.

Continue on up until you meet the asphalt road close to the OTE turn. Turn right and follow the road back up to the Old Village. If you wish to walk to Patitiri instead then 200m after turning right, turn left onto the dirt road which then crosses the donkey track. Turn left down the donkey track for Patitiri.

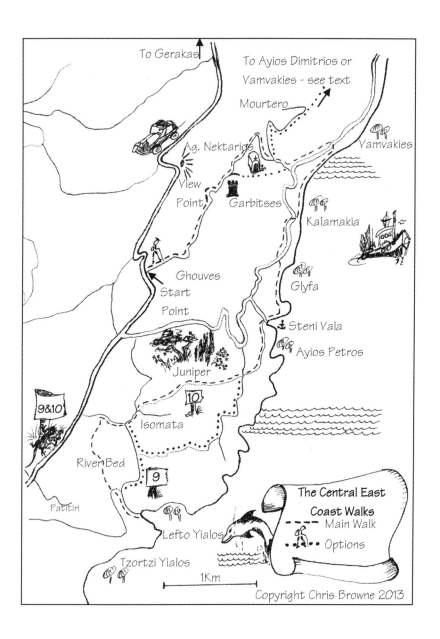

To Gerakas

To Ayios Dimitrios or
Vamvakies - see text

Mourtero

Ag. Nektarios

Vamvakies

View
Point

Garbitses

Kalamakia

Ghouves
Start
Point

Glyfa

Steni Vala

Ayios Petros

Juniper

9&10

10

Isomata

River Bed

9

Patitiri

Lefto Yialos

The Central East
Coast Walks
- - - Main Walk
···· Options

Tzortzi Yialos

1Km

Copyright Chris Browne 2013

64

The Central East Coast Walks

Walk 1: *Garbitses Archaeological Site - Vamvakies - Kalamakia - Glyfa Beach - Steni Vala*

Walk 2: *Steni Vala - Ayios Petros Bay - Isomata - Lefto Yialos Beach*

Distance Walk 1: 9 kms

Time Walk 1: 3-4 hours without stops

Distance Walk 2: 6 kms

Time Walk 2: 2-3 hours without stops

Swim Stop: Yes on both walks

Taverna: Yes. The tavernas at Lefto Yialos do not normally open until the beginning of June.

Walking shoes recommended. Shorts ok for most of the route but take long trousers or zip-offs. Take swimwear.

These routes will take you through a wide variety of scenery and make a wonderful 2 days' walking. Walk 1 can finish with a swim at Glyfa beach and lunch in one of the harbour side tavernas of Steni Vala, whilst walk 2 finishes at the lovely pebble beach of Lefto Yialos with a choice of 2 tavernas. The walk can also be made as one longer walk if you wish.

Walk 1 starts at Ghouves, which is roughly in the centre of Alonnisos. The route takes you through open countryside at high level with fabulous views to the islands of the marine park, and then along beautiful secluded beaches. On walk 2 the river bed section to Lefto Yialos beach through olive groves is one of the prettiest and most peaceful on Alonnisos.

Take the main road north along the island towards Gerakas and where the road divides with Steni Vala to the right, keep left and uphill. As you climb, the views out to the islands of the marine park open up and there is a parking area on the right of the road on a left hand bend. It's worth stopping if you can. Stop at the first right hand turn with a large industrial-looking building on the right. This area is called Ghouves. The building is the abattoir and worth avoiding in the run up to Easter.

Walk 1 starts here. Take the road off to the right which runs between olive groves and rough scrubland. After 2.2 kms you will see a sign on the right to Garbitses archaeological site. The path to the site follows the line of electricity poles. Garbitses was a fortified look out point and an impressive circular stone walled structure is still visible. From here there is a path which carries on down and re-joins the road below just by the turning to Mourtero. The path is steep and normally overgrown but it does cut off the last bend in the road. I always prefer to go back up to the road and turn right, the views are better anyway. Follow the road down and around to the right with views to the north across to Mourtero and onto Kyra Panagia. On your right you pass the little church of Ayios Nektarios. Continue down the road until a road joins to the left signposted to the small settlement of Mourtero.

If you wish to visit Mourtero you can turn left here, the walk around the valley is lovely and you will eventually pass a concrete road with a gate across it on the left and then a small kalivi with a new red roof on the right. Then as the road next bends to the left you will see a small driveway straight in front of you leading to a house with a small chapel in the garden. From here you can return to the main route or continue past a blue gate and a second house on the right. Continue on past two small tracks on the right and then turn right when you come to a junction. After 30 metres turn right then next left ignoring a track going down to the right (there is a large Agave plant on the right here and a view directly ahead to Vasiliko bay on Peristera island) Take the next turning down to the right where there is a short stone wall on your left and a track leading up to the left. Continue straight on and take the next left turn, where the track straight ahead drops down to the rear of a small hotel. Simply follow this track which goes more steeply downhill to join the main tarmac road along the island. Turn left for Ayios Dimitrios beach or right for Vamvakies and Kalamakia.

Carry on down the road until the next road junction and turn left here to Vamvakies.

You can continue straight on the road here for the direct route into Kalamakia.

Continue down to the *boatyard at Vamvakies* and have a look around. This is where most of the local caiques (work boats) are taken out for wintering and/or maintenance.

Turn around and head back along the road and as the road turns sharply up and left take the small footpath on the left of the bend next to a house. There is now a concrete parking space at this point. Follow this coastal path as it undulates between the sea and several houses. There are a few lovely small pebble beaches along this stretch. Eventually you will walk across the last pebble beach and be confronted with dark grey rocks. Carefully pick your way over the rocks and you will emerge on Kalamakia harbour. The earth bank on your right as you walk over the rocks is a very good place for fossil hunting.

Walk onto the quay and take the small track up from the back of the quay on your right and turn left where it joins the road on a sharp bend. Follow the road up the hill and around a sharp left then a sharp right bend. The

Poppies on a path in an olive grove, near Lefto Yialos beach

road levels out with the sea on your left. Follow the road along until you see a large house on a sharp bend on your right and a covered caravan below you to the left. Just past this on your left is a rough track leading down into the olive grove below. Follow the track down, around to the left at the bottom until you see the beach in front of you. Turn right onto a path just behind the beach and you will come out at one end of Glyfa beach. Carry on along the beach and straight up the road at the end. Ignore the turning to the right and carry straight on, the road goes past a church on the left and then turns into a small path. Follow the path past a small house on the left (there are usually lovely spring and autumn crocuses along here), over the headland and around to the right into Steni Vala harbour.

This is where walk 1 ends. A swim at Glyfa beach and lunch in Steni Vala is always a pleasure.

Walk 2 starts here. With the road onto the quay at Steni Vala joining on your right. Go straight ahead and turn left at the end past the MOM sanctuary (a small green hut) on your right. Continue on around the bay and you will soon arrive at the bay of Ayios Petros. Cross the beach and at the far side turn right up the footpath. At a junction in the path keep to the right and uphill until you come to a large new stone house where you must turn left. The path continues uphill and comes out at the end of a dirt road. Turn right and then take the first turn to the left.

See alternative routes from here at the end

Walk along this road a short way and you will see on your right a marker for footpath number 10 up to the village of Isomata. Take this path up to the right (the path is little more than a rocky goat track in most places). Stop every now and then to enjoy the ever changing views back across to Peristera Island. Eventually at the top the path goes between low juniper trees and past a large goat pen on your left. You will then come to a T-junction with a wider track. Turn right here, then left at the next T-junction with a main dirt road. Follow this road, around a bend to the right where there is a house on the corner with a sign for the "IKION" taverna. The road then bends sharply to the left, on the right of this corner are two cottages with an access road going in on the right. This is the continuation of path number 10 and is also part of path number 9. Take this access road into the right and almost immediately turn right again just past the second cottage. With this second cottage on your right and a stone wall to your left follow the path straight ahead along the right hand side of an olive grove and then down on the right into pine trees. At the bottom of this path you will cross a narrow gully.

The path on the far side of the gully is the continuation of paths 9 and 10 and continues uphill a short distance, then levels out. The path then crosses a dry stream bed, continues uphill and joins the main asphalt road visible above you.

You are now starting the dry river bed route to Lefto Yialos. This route is now paint spotted. Turn left just across the gully and follow the small path directly ahead until you reach a rocky dry river bed in front of you. Turn left and from here it is really a matter of following the river bed. Most of the way there is a slightly elevated path through olive groves alongside the river bed. After the first reasonably clear olive grove the river bed enters a wooded area. The river bed bends sharply left and then right. The easiest way through here is to follow the left bend in the river around the first left bend and then go straight ahead into the wooded area and immediately right between the trees. After just a few metres you re-join the river bed on your right. You will then come to an olive grove where the trees have been pruned back very hard. On the far side of this olive grove the path drops down to the left and crosses the river bed which has now narrowed, then continues across the next olive grove at an angle to the left. Follow this path across the olive grove and you will again drop down and cross the river bed. Once across the olive grove on the other side the route becomes a clear rocky road. Follow it down and where it joins a main road turn left for Lefto Yialos beach, past the marker on the left for path number 9 up to Isomata.

Alternative routes:

For an easier route underfoot than path 10 simply follow this road as it winds up to the village of Isomata. At the top where the road levels out you will pass a large new house on the right with a blue metal double gate across the drive. Just past this on the left is a marker for footpath number 9 which takes you down the hillside and emerges at a road junction where you turn left for Lefto Yialos beach. This is a steep direct route.

OR

To join the river bed route to Lefto Yialos continue past the sign for footpath number 9 and follow the road around to the right and between a few stone cottages and outbuildings. At the next sharp bend to the right there are two cottages directly in front of you with a small access road going in to the left. This is now marked paths 9 and 10. Turn left here and almost immediately right just past the second cottage. With this second cottage on your right and a stone wall to your left follow the path straight ahead along the right hand side of an olive grove and then down on the right into pine trees. *At the bottom of this path you will cross a narrow gully.*

Now follow the main route from this point.

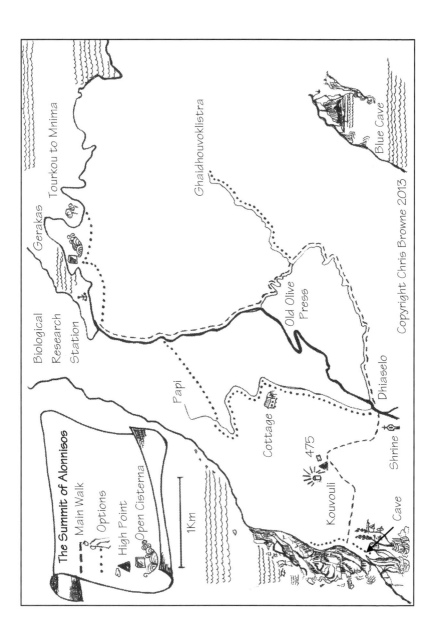

The Summit of Alonnisos

— — Main Walk
⋯⋯ Options
▲ High Point
Open Cisterna

1Km

Biological Research Station

Gerakas

Tourkou to Mnima

Ghaidhouvoklistra

Blue Cave

Papi

Old Olive Press

Dhiaselo

Cottage

475

Shrine

Kouvouli

Cave

Copyright Chris Browne 2013

The Summit of Alonnisos

Route: *Dhiaselo - Kouvouli Summit and the Coastal Cliffs – Gerakas – Tourkou Mnima*

Includes alternative route from Dhiaselo to Gerakas via Papi.

Distance: 12 kms

Time: 5-6 hours

Swim Stop: Yes

No Taverna

Footwear: Due to the terrain, boots or sturdy walking shoes are essential and you should take long trousers for the scratchy bits through cistus etc. (zip-offs are perfect).

This walk should present no problem to walkers of reasonable fitness but it does involve a fair amount of steep goat tracks and clambering over sharp stone faces towards the top, where there is now a weather antenna. At the time of writing this trail is not waymarked and involves following goat paths (I have now marked the route up Kouvouli with red paint spots). You will need to organise transport to get you to the start point of Dhiaselo (Διάσελο) and to pick you up again from Gerakas (Γέρακας) at the end of the island. To get to Dhiaselo head north along the island and turn left and uphill towards Gerakas at the junction where Steni Vala is shown to the right. Dhiaselo is 15 kms from Patitiri. If you do not wish to climb Kouvouli then the section described from Dhiaselo to Gerakas past the old olive press makes a nice gentle walk in itself. You can also just make the walk up to the summit for the views if you wish.

Without doubt, Kouvouli affords the best view on the island. It is the highest point on Alonnisos at 475m and on a clear day Mount Athos, the Halkidiki peninsula, Mount Olympus and Mount Parnassos are all visible as well as a panoramic view of all the islands in the Marine Park. If you ever get the chance to visit during the winter months when the visibility is always the best, then the view to these snow-capped mountains is truly wonderful.

Also described is how to go beyond the high point and across to the cliffs on the north west coast. The views back along the coast of Alonnisos towards the south and across to Skopelos, Evia and the mainland are as good as it gets.

At Dhiaselo you will find a small shrine on the left side of the road when facing north and on the right a trekking map at the start of path 11. Immediately behind the shrine is an olive grove, usually with an amazing array of goat watering containers! Head for these containers and follow the path past them up to the right and very quickly you will come to a rough track. Head straight across the track at this point to where the ground is mostly bare rock and follow the most obvious goat track straight ahead across the hillside.

The hillside here is covered in sea squills.

The route heads to the North across and up the slope most of the time. Remember this is also your route back down. Keep following the most obvious route as you traverse the hillside and don't be tempted to go up too quickly. Eventually after about 30 minutes you will see a large bare rock face above you to the left. Head straight to this rock face and go up it. At the top you will see a large stone cairn off to your right. The trig point marking the summit should now be visible up to your left. It is now just a case of heading straight for the summit which is best approached from the right as you look at it. From here your return to Dhiaselo is by the same route.

To continue to the north west coast cliffs, as you stand at the trig point looking out to Peristera island, turn right and head straight down over the rocks and, keeping right, you will come down into a small open clearing. Head straight across the clearing and up and out the other side. Turn 45 degrees to the left and follow the small path and after a few minutes turn left down into another small clearing. Turn right and walk through this clearing. You are now heading directly towards the cliffs although you will not see them yet. Follow the trail as it winds between the hollyoak trees and you will soon arrive at the cliffs. Once at the cliffs it is possible to walk fairly easily either left or right to explore for a short distance. Looking out to sea, if you go to the left and follow the goat track along the coastline you will find a cave below an old overhanging olive tree. Return to the trig point and then down to Dhiaselo the way you came.

From the shrine at Dhiaselo head towards Gerakas on the asphalt road. Immediately on your right are two dirt roads. Take the left and better-surfaced of these two roads towards Gerakas. As you follow this road you will walk through some of the prettiest olives groves on Alonnisos and past a number of traditional cottages (kalivis) used by the local people to live in whilst tending to their olive trees. After about 40 minutes you will come to a road going off up to the right.

This road to the right goes to an area called Ghaidhouroklistra and is a dead end but there are some fabulous views and wild country along here and a lovely old ruined cottage near the end with a marvellous fireplace inside. You can see this through the door but don't go inside as the floor is unsafe.

As you near re-joining the asphalt road you will see on your left the ruin of the old stone-built olive press with some of the machinery still visible inside. Continue down on to the asphalt road, where you turn right for the final stretch to Gerakas.

As you approach Gerakas you will see the Biological Research Station (a large white building) up to your left behind the beach.

*The Biological **Research** Station was funded by the Aga Khan's Bellerive foundation and opened by him personally to coincide with the establishment of the Marine Park. Sadly very little, if any, research has ever been carried out there.*

Gerakas does not have the prettiest beach on Alonnisos, but it's fine for a cooling swim and at the time of writing there has been a small kantina there for a few years which serves a simple but wonderful fresh fish lunch and cold drinks. If after all this you still have not had enough walking then there is an old goat track which runs around the right hand side of Gerakas bay and finishes at the rocks of the open sea coast at a place called Tourkou to Mnima or the Turkish Grave, a lovely place for a secluded picnic and from where there are wonderful views to the marine park islands.

To get there, just a few metres before you reach Gerakas bay on the asphalt road, there is the start of the goat track going up through the rocks on the right. The path is steep to begin with and then levels out. The path is marked with a few red spots along the way and you will pass a large open cisterna and small beach on your left after about 30 minutes. The path continues slightly uphill and to the right and finishes on the rocks of the open sea coast at Tourkou to Mnima. Return the same way to Gerakas.

Alternative route from Dhiaselo to Gerakas via Papi:

With the shrine at Dhiaselo on your left take the dirt road off to the left sign-posted Papi (Παπί). Continue along this road, through a gate and past the shepherd cottages on either side of the road. After a few minutes you will see a large corrugated tin goat encampment up to your left on the hill. As you approach the end of the road, and after about 3 kms from the start you will see a rough track going down on your right. This is an old agricultural access road and wider than just a path. Follow this track down towards the olive groves below. As you approach the olive groves you will come to a gate which is there to stop the goats from getting at the tender olive leaves so please make sure you close the gate behind you. Continue on down until you come out on the asphalt road and turn left for the final stretch to Gerakas harbour.

The view down to Gerakas from the high point of Kovouli

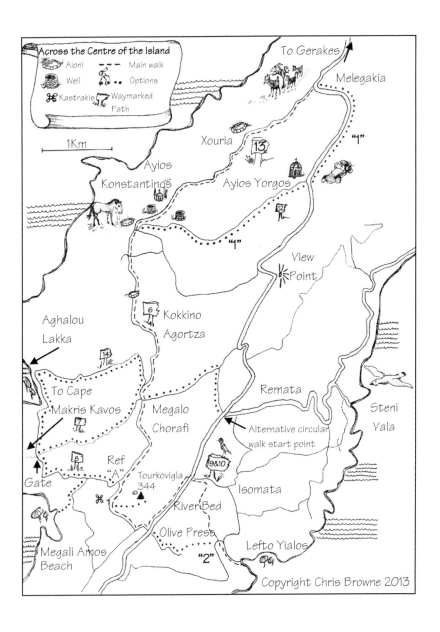

Across the Centre of the Island

Aloni
Well
Kastrakis

Main walk
Options
Waymarked Path

1Km

To Gerakes
Melegakia
Xouria
13
Ayios Konstantinos
Ayios Yorgos
12
"1"
View Point
Aghalou Lakka
6
Kokkino Agortza
14
To Cape
Makris Kavos
Remata
Steni Vala
Megalo Chorafi
Alternative circular walk start point
Ref "A"
Gate
9&10
Tourkovigla 344
Isomata
River Bed
Olive Press
Lefto Yialos
Megali Amos Beach
"2"

Copyright Chris Browne 2013

78

Across the Centre of the Island

Main Route: *Melegakia – Xouria - Ayios Konstantinos - Kokkino Agortza - Megalo Chorafi - Kastraki - Lefto Yialos Beach*

Distance: 14 kms

Time: 4.5 to 5.5 hours without stops

Swim Stop: Yes

Taverna: Yes at Lefto Yialos, open normally from the beginning of June

Walking shoes recommended. Shorts ok for most of the route but take long trousers or zip-offs for the scratchy bits. Take swimwear.

If I had to choose a favourite walk, this would be it. I have included many possible variations so that you can enjoy this wonderful part of Alonnisos many times over. These include a shorter circular route from Melegakia to Ayios Yorgos via Ayios Konstantinos, Cape Makris Kavos for fantastic snorkelling, the remote beaches of Aghalou Lakka and Megali Amos, plus a walk up the 2nd highest point on Alonnisos, Tourkovigla. As always there are ups and downs but generally this is not too taxing a walk.

Megalo Chorafi (big field) is at the centre of some wonderful walking country. The main route described goes from Melegakia in the north to the small shepherds' settlement and church of Ayios Konstantinos, then onto Megalo Chorafi and the ancient hill top fortification of Kastraki before finally crossing the island to finish at Lefto Yialos beach.

Any of the walks which pass through Megalo Chorafi can be accessed easily from Remata on the main asphalt road going north along Alonnisos (see map). The route from Remata up to Megalo Chorafi is, in itself, a very pleasant walk on a small gravel road and will take about 1 hour. On the way up there is one junction where you keep left and uphill (to the right will eventually take you back to the asphalt road farther north). This road is a particularly good place to see the abundant nests of the pine processionary moth (like small brown bird's nests) hanging all over the pine trees. In spring the ground is covered with long lines of their caterpillars, joined nose to tail, as they forage for food. The hairs of these caterpillars are an extreme irritant so DO NOT TOUCH. From Megalo Chorafi you can make a circular walk down to the west coast. See alternative routes.

To get to the start point: take the main road north along the island towards Gerakas and just past Remata and around an S bend the road divides with Steni Vala to the right and Gerakas uphill to the left. Take the road up to Gerakas. As you climb the views out to the islands of the marine park open up and there is a parking area on the right of the road on a left hand bend. It's worth stopping. You will notice that as you progress northwards the pine forests die out and are replaced by lower macchia vegetation. After 6.5 kms you will come to a sharp right hand bend in the road with a map of the walks on the left hand side. Just past the bend on the left is a large parking area. This is Melegakia.

The walk starts here with the large map on your right shoulder. This is the beginning of path number 13 and there are waymarkers all along the route until you reach Ayios Konstantinos. Follow the path alongside a dry river bed and past many holm oak trees, tree heather, and an abundance of strawberry trees. There are also many crocuses here in spring. The path will lead you through two small circular bare fields (Lakka) which is where wheat used to be grown in years gone by and, in the springtime, these fields are now covered in chamomile and patches of wild mint.

After about 40 minutes you will come to a place where there is a huge carob tree on the left hand side and off to your right slightly uphill is an old aloni (threshing floor). Turn right here and walk the short distance up to the aloni through the cistus (rock roses) that covers the ground and enjoy the sea views (it'll be cistus leaves that you pick from your socks at the end of the day!).

This place is called Xouria and you will see many ruined dwellings scattered around. Return to the large carob tree and with this on your left go straight ahead and follow the path, which soon becomes little more than a goat track crossing many small ravines until you arrive at a fenced area in front of you. This is just a large goat corral. Go through the gate (closing it behind you) and follow the path down to the left, past an outbuilding on the left (this area is a sea of anemones in the spring) and on up past the many holly oak trees (the wood from which, when pliable, is used to fashion the yolks around the goats necks for the bells) to the gate on the other side of the corral. Shortly after leaving the corral you will begin a sharp descent to the church of Ayios Konstantinos. From this point you will be able to look down and see the rough road on the other side of the valley which is the continuation of your walk. Continue on down taking special care as this section can be loose underfoot and you will come to the church at the bottom.

You will find a table in the shade of a very large mulberry tree just past the church. On the terrace below the table there are many dark brown arum lilies. Leave your things here for a moment and walk back through the gate to the church courtyard. The church has the key in the door if you wish to take a look. Take the gate out of the courtyard on the far side and enjoy the view down the valley to the sea. On May 21st the route you are about to take up the hill away from the church is teeming with all the Kostas, Dinas and Elenis on the island as they visit the church to celebrate their name day.

Take the hill up from the church, past one of the two wells here on the left. In spring the olive groves on the left here are some of the prettiest around, covered in wild gladioli and tassel and grape hyacinths.

At the top of the hill you will come to an aloni on your right. The road to the right leads to the homes of the few shepherds who live here (one of the shepherds still carves lovely wooden spoons from holly oak). Straight ahead the path continues to the right of a large trekking map, and off to your right is a view to the islet of Manolas.

There is a lovely circular route from here to the church of Ayios Yorgos and then back to Melegakia. See option 1

Continue on the path and at the picnic table on the right after just a minute or so turn back to enjoy the view of the shepherds' houses. Follow the path marked with red spots on the rocks along and across a dirt road. The next landmark to look out for is a paved aloni which the path crosses and then you will come to the area called Kokkino Agortza (wild red pear trees). Here there are several ruined dwellings and fabulous views across to Skopelos. Continue on the path and you will come into a small open field where you turn right and follow the path over a low terrace wall and into the trees. You eventually emerge at Megalo Chorafi with a shaded seat on your left, a ruined cottage further to the left and a shepherd's cottage below you to the right where the rough approach road ends. The view across to the islands of Dio Adelphia through the pine trees from here is fabulous.

Our main walking route now continues down path 8 to Kastraki and across to Lefto Yialos beach on the east coast. There are, however, two alternative routes to the west coast from Megalo Chorafi. These are:

A. Megalo Chorafi to the coast road and Aghalou Lakka beach.

B. Megalo Chorafi to the coast road with an option to cape Makris Kavos-a fantastic snorkelling spot, and/or the main pebble beach of Megali Amos bay.

Both these options are described in detail after the main walk.

Head off on the road to your right, past the large trekking route map, and immediately on the right is the paved beginning of walk number 14 down to the beach of Aghalou Lakka on the west coast. Continue on the road and as the road bends to the left you will see the start of walk number 7, also down to the west coast. Continue past this and almost immediately on your right you will see the start of path number 8. Turn right onto this path and follow it down through the trees. You will come to an olive grove where the path turns left then sharp right alongside a stone wall and across the olive grove. You re-enter the trees and continue left along the path which is spotted with paint marks. The path takes you through another olive grove and continues downhill, criss-crossing a small valley through trees. After a few minutes keep a look out for a path going up to your left. There is a red spot marker on a large stone in the middle of the path, across which there is a fallen pine tree. **This is reference point A.**

Take this path off to the left (straight ahead takes you down to the west coast) and follow it up until it emerges at the end of a rough dirt track. Above you on your right is the archaeological site of Kastraki, an ancient fortified hill-top look-out point. Just after you meet the track there is a reasonably flat olive grove on your right. This makes for a shady rest stop and a chance to explore Kastraki. If you do wish to explore then as you turn right into the olive grove, with the hill of Kastraki on your right, walk along the edge of the hill until you see the most obvious goat track going up and follow it to the top. The views are well worth it. Leaving Kastraki behind follow the track up until you come to a junction with another track.

From here you can make a detour to the top of Tourkovigla, the 2nd highest point on Alonnisos at 344m. Turn left here and follow the road around as it bears right and finishes at an olive grove above a partly finished stone wall on the left. Follow the red spot markers and the small stone cairns left by other walkers up to the left through the olive grove, then rough undergrowth, until you reach the concrete trig point at the top. Simply relax and enjoy the stunning panoramic views over both sides of the island. Return down the same way and continue straight past the track on the right from Kastraki.

Keep straight ahead and you will soon come to a T-junction with a dirt road where there is a new house on the right hand corner. The view down to Kokkino Kastro and the islet of Kokkinonisi from here is wonderful. Turn left here and the road starts to drop down and to the right to join the asphalt road at a 4 way junction.

See option 2 for the direct forest trail to Lefto Yialos beach from here.

Turn left here and walk along the tarmac road. After 1.8 kms on your right you will see a trekking map and stone steps leading down to the right. Take this path, number 9 and 10, down and as you bear right at the bottom and start walking on part of the rocky river bed notice the path which goes up to the left (normally marked by a red arrow on a rock) and between some bushes. This is the waymarked path up to the village of Isomata. Continue past this left turn and along the river bed and then left across an olive grove which cuts off the next left bend in the river bed. Now it is simply a matter of following the river bed. Most of the way there is a slightly elevated path through olive groves alongside the river bed. After the first reasonably clear olive grove the river bed enters a wooded area. The river bed bends sharply left and then right. The easiest way through here is to follow the left bend in the river around and then go straight ahead into the

wooded area and immediately right between the trees. After just a few metres you re-join the river bed on your right. You will then come to an olive grove where the trees have been pruned back very hard. On the far side of this olive grove the path drops down to the left and crosses the river bed which has now narrowed, then continues across the next olive grove at an angle to the left. Follow this path across the olive grove and

Cliff face close to Tourkoneri beach

you will again drop down and cross the river bed. Once across the olive grove on the other side the route becomes a clear rocky road. Follow it down and where it joins a main road turn left for Lefto Yialos beach, past the marker on the left for path number 9 up to Isomata.

Option 1: Circular Route – Melegakia – Ayios Konstantinos – Ayios Yorgos – Melegakia. Turn left here and then left again onto waymarked path number 12 which will take you to the church of Ayios Yorgos (one starting point for the gorge walk). The route is fairly straightforward; you start with the coast visible for some time to your left and then head right up through a wooded valley. Although there are several tracks which cross your route along the way just keep to the main path. As you climb the hill you will pass through a bare circular area where crops were grown (Lakka) and then continue through the trees to an olive grove where there is a picnic table to your right. With the picnic table on your right follow the path straight ahead (there is a kalivi on your left). From here the path is flanked on both sides by abundant strawberry trees. At the end you will come to a gravel parking area with a great view and the road below you. Down to your left is the church of Ayios Yorgos which is open. There is a spring just off to the right of the church. You can turn left on the asphalt road and walk back to your start point at Melegakia. This makes a very nice circular walk.

Option 2: The forest trail to Lefto Yialos Beach. Go straight across the crossroads and follow the road along, ignoring all side turnings. You will pass the island's community olive press on the left. Follow the road until it comes to a dead end with access to a house on your right. Opposite this on your left you will find a rough path going into the undergrowth. Follow this in and after a few metres you will be free of the undergrowth and on a forest path. Turn right and follow this path as it winds down through the forest. Towards the bottom you will see open olive groves across to your left. The path you are on carries on down but tends to become overgrown near the bottom due to lack of use. Turn right at the bottom and you will come out at a junction with the road leading to Lefto Yialos beach. Turn left here to the beach.

These are the 2 alternative routes to the west coast from Megalo Chorafi.

A. Megalo Chorafi to the coast road and Aghalou Lakka beach. Down path 14, return path 7.

B. Megalo Chorafi to the coast road with an option to cape Makris Kavos- a fantastic snorkelling spot and/or the main pebble beach of Megali Amos bay. Down path 7, return path 8.

A. From Megalo Chorafi head off towards the road on your right, past the large trekking route map on the right, and immediately on the right is the paved beginning of walk number 14 down to the beach of Aghalou Lakka. Take this path to the right. This route is steep and takes at least one hour. When you get to the bottom you will join the coast road. Turn left and look for the small path on the right next to a fence down through the olive trees to the beach of Aghalou Lakka. When you come up from the beach turn right and follow the coast road around the bay until you meet a large gate across the road. Just before the gate on the left is the paved start of walk number 7 which is also steep and takes you back up to Megalo Chorafi. It takes about 2 hours. This walk makes a nice circular route.

B. From Megalo Chorafi head off towards the road on your right, past the large trekking route map on the right, and immediately on the right is the paved beginning of walk number 14 down to the beach of Aghalou Lakka (as in alternative A above).

Continue on the road and as the road bends to the left you will see the start of walk number 7 on your right down to the coast. Take this path to the right and down to the coast, which will take you about 1 hour and 30 minutes. Where you meet the coast road there is a gate on the left and a track directly opposite you. This is the start of the way down to Cape Makris Kavos, a large promontory which is a favourite fishing spot for locals and a fantastic snorkelling spot.

The way to cape Makris Kavos: head down the track opposite you and after about 50m turn right then immediately left through the olive trees. In front of you is a fenced area with a gate in it. Go through the gate, closing it behind you, and straight ahead past a collection of watering troughs for the goats. From here follow the rough path ahead and slightly to the right as it drops down into pine trees. You will see the cape below you. Follow the path down through the pine trees and out onto the cape. Along the cape there are many spots to the left where you can climb down to the sea. The water here is deep and great for snorkelling but beach shoes are a must for getting out of the water without injuring your feet.

Turn left through the gate and continue on the coast road.

The way to Megali Amos beach: shortly after passing through the gate you will come to a new house on the right. Immediately before this house on the right there is a new path signposted down to Megali Amos beach. Take this path down until you meet a dirt road. Turn right along the road and after just a few metres you will find the continuation of the path down to the beach on your left. Return the same way (as an alternative you can return the same way until you meet the first dirt road, where you turn right. Keep on this road and take the first turn on the left which will take you back towards the gate. The start of walk number 8 will now be on your right).

You will then come to the paved start of walk number 8 on your left up to Megalo Chorafi (steep and about 1 hour 30 minutes).

You can take a short detour on the way up to visit the archaeological site of Kastraki.

Follow this path up and after about 10 minutes you will come to a rough gate which you simply go through and re-tie behind you. Then after about 20 minutes fom the road keep a lookout for a red spot marker on a large stone in the middle of the path, across which there is a fallen pine tree. **This is reference point A as described in the main walk.**

If you wish to visit Kastraki then turn right here and follow the instructions detailed earlier in the main walk down from Megalo Chorafi. Return to reference point A, turn right and continue up to Megalo Chorafi.

If you do not wish to visit Kastraki simply continue straight on up the path to Megalo Chorafi.

View down to the south coast -
close to the Old Schoolhouse in the Old Village

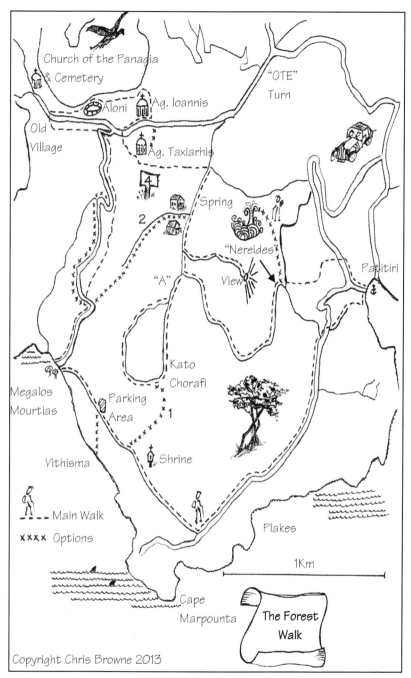

Church of the Panagia & Cemetery

Aloni

Ag. Ioannis

"OTE" Turn

Old Village

Ag. Taxiarhis

4

2

Spring

"Nereides"

"A"

View

Patitiri

Kato Chorafi

Megalos Mourtias

Parking Area

1

Vithisma

Shrine

— Main Walk

xxxx Options

Plakes

1Km

Cape Marpounta

The Forest Walk

Copyright Chris Browne 2013

90

The Forest Walk

Main Route: *Patitiri – Paliochorafina - Kato Chorafi Forest - Old Village - Megalos Mourtias Beach – Patitiri*

If starting from the Old Village you can use these instructions to visit the nearby churches of Ayios Ioannis and Ayios Taxiarhis and make the walk to Megalos Mourtias beach and into Patitiri.

Distance: 11 kms

Time: 3-4 hours without stops

Swim Stop: Yes

Taverna: Yes at Megalos Mourtias

Walking shoes or boots recommended. Shorts ok for most of the route but take zip-offs or long trousers. Take swimwear.

This moderately easy walk takes you quickly out of Patitiri and on a lovely circular route around the forest of Kato Chorafi. You will visit a wonderful view point over Patitiri and along the coast and then the small church of Ayios Ioannis, with a short optional detour to the church of Ayios Taxiarhis. When you reach the Old Village there is a short optional walk included, or you may decide to explore at your leisure on another day. The walk continues down to Megalos Mourtias beach and then back along the coastal route into Patitiri with an option to visit the secluded beach of Vithisma along the way.

With your back to the sea in Patitiri take the left-hand road away from the harbour. Ignore the first road on the left and carry on past the tourist shops and two supermarkets on the left. Immediately past the second supermarket there is a small path to the left, which quickly turns into wide stone steps. On the opposite side of the road at this point is a steep concrete ramp. Follow these steps up and around several bends. Eventually the steps finish and you turn left up a concrete footpath, at the end of which you turn right onto a concrete road. The views over Patitiri harbour area from here are impressive. Walk up this road, past a small church on the left, and you come to a T-junction directly opposite the Nereides Hotel which, perhaps unexpectedly, is a great place to eat with real home made wine and fantastic home made dolmades and fresh samphire (kritama). This area is called Paliochorafina. Turn left here and then immediately right up the side of the hotel.

If you turned right here and then kept left at the only junction, you will emerge at the spring on the donkey track between Patitiri and the Old Village.

Then take the first left and follow this road up and take the first right turn which goes sharply uphill and into the start of the pine forest.

Follow the road up, past a new house on the left and then a pair of old cottages also on the left. Here the road bends sharply left (on the right are the gates to a new house). Follow the road around to the left and after about 20m you will be faced with a junction with a forest track directly ahead or a right turn on the road.

Take the right turn and follow the road which starts going downhill. Follow this road down to a 4 way junction with other forest roads. **This is reference point** A.

Take the road to the left which soon heads uphill. At the top of the hill you will see a house on your right at the bottom of a rough concrete drive.

A little further on and you come to a point where a road joins from the right. This is the **start of a circular walk (see option 1)** through the forest and olive groves. Keep straight ahead, ignore all side turnings and follow the road down and around in a rough circle to the right and you will return to your start point. There are wonderful views up to the Old Village from sections of this circular route and fabulous views across to Skopelos, beyond the islets of Mikro and Ayios Yorgos.

There is a small church and the remains of a monastery on Ayios Yorgos. When you travel to Skopelos the boats usually take the route between Ayios Yorgos and Skopelos. As you pass take a look at the side of Ayios Yorgos facing Skopelos and you will first see the small white church and then the old stone walls of the monastery to the right. Directly below is a small jetty from where there is a path up to the church.

From this part of Kato Chorafi there is an alternative way down to the beach of Megalos Mourtias with the opportunity to visit Vrithisma beach on the way.

The harbour at Patitiri

To continue with the main walk return to the 4-way junction at reference point A and continue straight ahead and downhill. After a few minutes you will come to a turning on the right. Take this right turn and follow the road past the new football club on the left and after a few minutes you come to a point where there is a new house on your right. From here there are wonderful views over Patitiri and along the coast of Alonnisos.

Straight ahead and slightly left are the islands of the Two Brothers (about 5 miles), then Skantzoura (about 12 miles) and Skyros (about 35 miles). To the right is the profile of northern Evia (Evia being the second largest island in Greece - sadly recently devastated by the fires of summer 2007), the extreme left hand side of which is the port of Kymi, also about 35 miles distant. The mountain you see is Mount Dirfus at 1750m. On a very clear day to the left of Kymi the island of Andros is also visible.

Return the same way past the football club and turn right. You will come to two large new villas with swimming pools on the left. In between the villas is the old dirt road leading down to Megalos Mourtias beach. *If you wish to take this route see option 2.*

Continue past these two new villas on the left, then more new houses on the right and you will soon reach the spot where the old donkey track from Patitiri to the Old Village crosses the road you are on.

There is a wonderful view up to the Old Village from here with the Kastro (castle) at the top. Beyond is the peak of Kalovoulos, the 3rd highest point on Alonnisos. You can make the walk up Kalovoulos, see "The Old Village and Beyond" walk. The lower new part of the village is often referred to locally as "Little England".

Turn left onto the paved donkey track and follow it until it joins the main asphalt road. Turn right and head down hill for a few hundred metres until you see a large black metal gate on your left at the bottom of a dirt track.

A short detour to visit the church of Ayios Taxiarhis. Continue down the asphalt road for another 15 metres and then take the small concrete road up on the right towards a gate. Turn right up the steps just before a fence and continue on the path to the church. Return the same way.

Turn left through the gate and left again at the top (notice the cross on the rock above you to the left). Now simply follow the path along past the church of Ayios Ioannis (a good spot to stop and watch the bee-eaters in early summer) along an old stone path and directly down onto the aloni (threshing floors). From the aloni you have wonderful views along the south west coast of Alonnisos, to the islet of Manolas and in the foreground the rock of Stavros (crucifix) rising from the sea.

According to local folklore God put Stavros where it is to protect the people of Alonnisos from the devils that were believed to inhabit Manolas. From here if you look beyond Manolas on a clear day you will see Mount Athos.

From the aloni continue straight on up the asphalt road and at the top of the short hill turn left into the main entrance of the Old Village. The bus stop is on your right.

A short walk through the Old Village: with the bus stop on your right walk up the road to the plateia (square) at the top. On your left is the 17th century Church of Christ. Follow the steps up to the left around the back of the church (the door into the church is usually open. It is unusual in that is has a gallery for women to worship). You will come to a small terrace with a café and a great view. On your right take the path up and past the memorial to nine islanders who were shot by the Nazis on the 15th August 1944 during the festival of Panagia. Continue ahead past the old doorway, a small village house recently restored as a museum and

With the bus stop on your right walk up towards the Old Village and after about 50m you come to Fantasia house and Despina's shop on your left. Immediately before Fantasia house turn left down a path and then left again onto the road it joins at the bottom. Follow the road along past a few houses on your right and you will come to a junction where the road bears left. Go straight across here and down some steep stone steps which lead onto an asphalt road at the bottom. Turn right here and follow the road past the last few houses and around a right hand bend. You can either continue on this road all the way to the beach or look for a painted stone marking a path going off to the left on this bend. Follow this path down past bushes and then pine trees until you reach a house with a tennis court. The path goes left here and almost immediately down to the right and re-joins the asphalt road. Turn left and follow the road down to Megalos Mourtias beach.

At the beach, with the sea on your right, walk up the steps at the end of the beach and turn right onto the dirt road. Follow the road around to the left and then uphill. As you go up the hill you will come to a small turning/ parking area on your left.

The way down to Vithisma Beach: opposite the parking area is a rough dirt road going down towards the sea. Follow this road down and turn right onto a path at the bottom to the beach.

Continue along this lovely section of coastal road and past a shrine in the trees to your left.

The inscription on this shrine reads "Here Georgios Andreas Tsoumas accidentally fell and was saved by Germans in the year 1944. The Saints be praised."

At the end of this road you come to a T-junction with an asphalt road. Here you turn left and follow the road back into Patitiri.

Option 1: alternative route from Kato Chorafi Forest to Megalos Mourtias Beach. From the **circular walk start point**, turn right and follow the road around a bend to the left, down through pine trees and around to the right. The road now goes through a small rough olive grove, around to the left and through more pine trees, ignoring two small right turns. After about 100m from this last bend you will come to a small clearing on the right amongst the pine trees. Turn right here and follow the path down until you emerge with a fantastic view of Cape Marpounta from the top of an olive grove. It is not uncommon to see dolphins swimming around this cape from here. At the bottom of the olive grove is the coast road to Megalos Mourtias beach. Go left and downhill through the olive grove. Turn right about half way down near some old stone walls and continue down to the road. Turn right for the beaches of Vithisma and Megalos Mourtias or left for Patitiri.

Option 2: this is the old road down to Megalos Mourtias beach and emerges on the new asphalt road a few hundred metres back from the beach. On the way down you pass one of the largest umbrella pine trees on the island, the type of tree from which pine nuts are harvested. When you reach the asphalt road turn left for the beach. Walk along the back of the beach and up the stone steps to the dirt road at the top where you turn right to Vithisma beach and Patitiri.

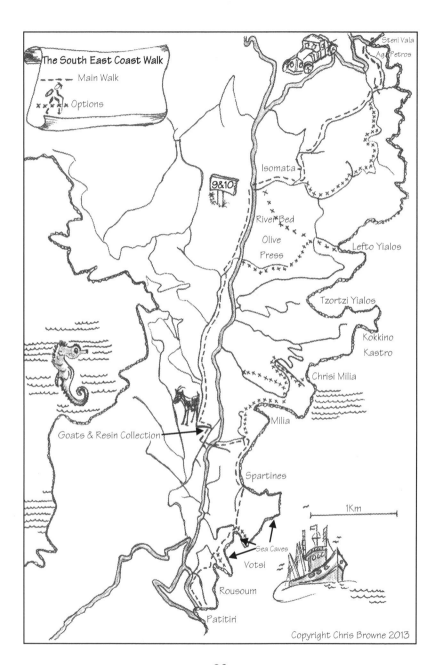

The South East Coast Walk

- - - Main Walk
×××× Options

9&10

Isomata

River Bed

Olive

Press

Steni Vala
Ag. Petros

Lefto Yialos

Tzortzi Yialos

Kokkino
Kastro

Chrisi Milia

Milia

Goats & Resin Collection

Spartines

1Km

Sea Caves

Votsi

Rousoum

Patitiri

Copyright Chris Browne 2013

98

The South East Coast Walk

Main Route: *Patitiri – Rousoum – Votsi – Spartines – Isomata - Ayios Petros - Steni Vala*

Includes optional routes out to Rousoum Headland, Votsi Beach and Sea Cave, Milia and Chrisi Milia Beaches and Lefto Yialos Beach via the forest route. Also includes an alternative easier route from Isomata to Ayios Petros

Distance: 15 kms

Time: 5-6 hours without stops

Swim Stop: Yes

Taverna: Yes at Rousoum, Votsi and Steni Vala.

Walking shoes recommended. Shorts ok for most of the route but take long trousers or zip-offs for the scratchy bits. Take swimwear.

> *This route will give you a wonderful day's walking through coastal fishing villages and open countryside. If you leave Patitiri in the morning you will arrive at the lovely harbour of Steni Vala in time for a refreshing swim and a relaxing lunch. You can return by bus or taxi.*

Follow the 10 km marathon walk up from Patitiri harbour, past the fire station on the left and stop at the crossroads.

Go straight across the crossroads and after about 50m turn right onto a small concrete road. Follow the road around to the left and then down to the right as it turns into stone steps which go down the side of the Gorgona Hotel. Follow the steps down, across a concrete road and onto one end of Rousoum beach. Walk straight along the back of the beach and up the stone steps which face you at the far end where the road joins from the left.

Rousoum Headland: if you wish to take the path out over the headland then turn right after just a few steps up, go up a few more steps then follow the path along the coast, past a house and a low stone wall. At the end of the path you will come to a small shed: take the path to the right to go down onto the rocks. Return the same way.

At the top follow the road around to the right along the coast, past a new hotel on the right. Just around the next left bend there is a set of steps going down on the right. Go down these steps, across the café terrace of Pension Dimitris, and down more steps to Votsi harbour. After you have had a look around take the road up from the harbour and around a right hand bend. The next bend is a sharp left and on the right hand side of this bend there is a traffic mirror and a concrete road going off to the right. Turn right on this road.

Votsi sea cave

Votsi Beach and Sea Cave: a little way along this road on the right are the steps down to Votsi beach. If you walk to the end of the road, past two tavernas on the left, it turns into a small path leading straight ahead through the forest. At the end you come to a cliff edge overlooking the sea. If you turn right just before the cliff edge and head down through the pine trees you come to the harbour mole (sea defence wall) from where you can swim on the open sea side into the cave just outside.

There is a building on your left, turn left and uphill immediately past this building. You walk up here with the building on your left and after just a few metres you will come out onto the bottom of a road with houses on the left. Continue up a short distance and on the right as the road bears left you will see the entrance through an archway into the grounds of the Hotel Panorama. Go through the archway and almost immediately turn left up the path, keeping the hotel on your right, and you will come to a gravel parking area. Go straight across to the entrance into the parking area, where you meet a road. On the opposite side of the road and slightly to the left you will see a small path leading downhill to the left.

To the right is a small outbuilding with a house further to the right. In the outbuilding is a working loom operated by Tassia. If she is there she will normally be happy to show you the rugs and other things she has made and perhaps let you buy something.

Follow this path down to the left until it joins a rough road. Turn right down this road and right again just before the house at the end and down onto Spartines beach. With your back to the sea go to the far right hand side of the beach and take the path up which carries on from the beach along the cliff edge. Continue on this path along the coast and through pine trees to another smaller beach with a large circular stone clad hole at the back of the beach. The hole has half an old boat and sadly normally rubbish in it. This is one of the old lime kilns, where the lime for asvesti (whitewash) was extracted from the rocks.

With your back to the sea head straight off the back of the beach and slightly right down and across a small gully. The path heads uphill and slightly left from here through the pine trees (look for the red spots), and comes out to join a rough road at the top. Turn left here at a fence and walk to the end where it joins the asphalt road.

To visit the beaches of Milia (apple trees) and Chrisi Milia (golden apple trees). Turn back to your right signposted to Milia Bay and simply follow this road past the football pitch on the right, Milia Bay Hotel on the right (a great place for lunch around the pool) and all the way down to the beach. When on the beach facing the sea turn left up the steep concrete ramp and at the top where there is a gate across the road, go to the left behind the fence and straight ahead. Past the fence you re-join a rough dirt access road and then an asphalt road. Turn right* and follow the road down (Chrisi Milia beach is below you to the right). At the bottom there is a right turn which leads you to the beach. A further diversion: *just a few metres after making this right turn you will see a track going up to your left. The track goes uphill through rough undergrowth, then through olive groves (there are two very big houses on your right) and re-joins the asphalt road near the main road along the island. There are some nice views along here.

Turn left here and follow the asphalt road a short distance until you see a turning on your right with a traffic mirror (to the left of the turning is a builder's yard). Turn right and right again at the T-junction in front of you where there is a trekking map. As you walk along here you pass the resin collection point on the left in front of an old goat encampment.

Immediately past here follow the road around to the left, uphill and then around to the right (there is a road going in on the left of this bend which is a private drive). Continue on this road past the next left turn signposted to Aghii Anargiri. About 15 minutes past this turn you will come to a new mini development of houses with pools on your right (to the left of these when looking out to sea are the stone remains of an old church) and the road bears to the left with a smaller dirt road going off up to the right.

Take this road up to the right and continue along it, ignoring all side turnings. Towards the end you will pass a left turn (the views down to the headland of Kokkino Kastro [red castle] from here are stunning), keep straight ahead and the road starts to drop down and around to the right to join the asphalt road at a 4 way junction.

Lefto Yialos beach via the forest route. Go straight across here and follow the road, ignoring all side turnings. You will pass the island's community olive press on the left. Follow the road until it comes to a dead end with access to a house on your right. Opposite this on your left you will find a rough path going into the undergrowth. Follow this in and after a few metres you will be free of the undergrowth and on a forest path. Turn right and follow this path as it winds down through the forest. Towards the bottom you will see open olive groves across to your left. The path you are on does carry on down but tends to become a bit overgrown near the bottom due to lack of use. Turn right at the bottom and make your way along a rough road to join the main road leading to Lefto Yialos beach. Turn left here to the beach.

Turn left here and walk along the tarmac road. After 1.8 kms on your right you will see a trekking map and stone steps leading down to the right. This is the start of paths 9 and 10. Take this path down and, as you bear right at the bottom, you start walking on part of a dry rocky river bed. Take the path which goes up to the left (normally marked by a red spot) and between some bushes.

Note: if you continue along the river bed and follow it around to the left you will join the river bed route down to Lefto Yialos as described in the "The Central East Coast" walk.

Follow the path along and down across a small gully. Across the gully the path winds uphill from the left, through olive then pine trees, and comes out at the top in an olive grove. Turn left here and follow the path along the side of a cottage. Turn left past the cottage and you join a dirt road on a bend. This is the village of Isomata.

Alternative easier route to Ayios Petros: Turn right and simply follow this road all the way down towards Ayios Petros and Steni Vala, re-joining the main route*.

Turn left and follow this road past a cottage on the left with an "Ikion" taverna sign hanging outside. Go around the bend to the left and take the first right turn which is path number 10. Follow this dirt road around to the right and then on your left the path leaves the road and goes across rough ground and behind and to the left of a goat enclosure. Just follow the path and it eventually starts to drop down through a low forest of juniper trees towards the coast.

From here there are wonderful views across to Peristera and its small lighthouse, to the right of which you will see a collection of small white buildings right on the rocks. This is the base from where archaeologists dive over a shipwreck discovered just off the coast. This wreck is historically one of the most significant ever found in the Aegean, dating from around 470BC and containing more than 3000 amphorae (most of which are still on the wreck). The significance of the wreck was, however, due to its size more than its cargo. Until the discovery of this wreck historians believed that the Greeks and Romans were building ships of no more than 15m in length around the 5th century BC. This wreck was measured at more than 25m in length and 10m wide.

Continue down the path and you will join a dirt road at the bottom, where you turn left.

***If you have taken the alternative easier route from Isomata you join here.**

Follow the road along and take the first turn to the right and where the road ends in a turning area take the path down to the left towards a large new stone house to the right of a rough access driveway. Follow this path down to the beach at Ayios Petros bay. Turn left across the beach and follow the path up from the far end, around the headland and down into Steni Vala past the MOM monk seal rehabilitation centre.

Congratulations! Steni Vala is a great place to relax for a while with a beer and watch the boats come and go. It is never too long before one of the visiting sailing boats fouls the anchor line of one of the local fishing caiques when trying to leave, and pandemonium breaks out. Great fun if you're not involved!

If you would like a swim first then you can walk along the harbour, past all the tavernas and cafés, and follow the small path around and over the headland to the lovely white pebble beach of Glyfa, just 10 minutes walk from Steni Vala.

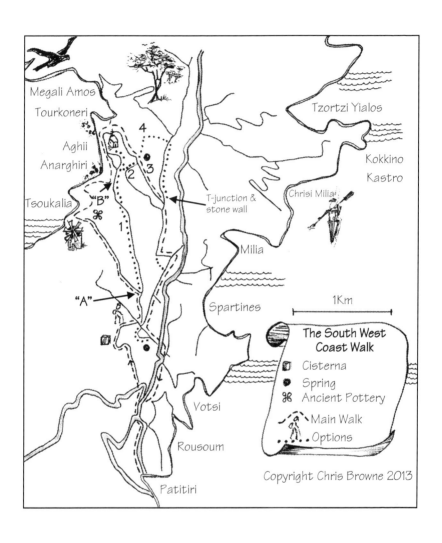

Megali Amos

Tourkoneri

Aghii
Anarghiri

Tsoukalia

"B"

4

3

2

1

T-junction &
stone wall

Tzortzi Yialos

Kokkino
Kastro

Chrisi Milia

Milia

"A"

Spartines

1Km

The South West
Coast Walk

Cisterna
Spring
Ancient Pottery

Main Walk
Options

Votsi

Rousoum

Patitiri

Copyright Chris Browne 2013

106

The South West Coast Walk

Main Route: *Patitiri — Tsoukalia Beach and Archaeological Site — Aghii Anarghiri — Tourkoneri Beach - Patitiri*

Includes Alternative Return Routes

Distance: 12 kms

Time: 4-5 hours without stops

Swim Stop: Yes

No Taverna

Walking shoes recommended. Shorts ok. Take swimwear.

> On the north west side of Alonnisos, 5.5 kms from Patitiri, lies the beach of Tsoukalia, one of several designated archaeological sites on the island. The two small chapels of Aghii Anarghiri are situated on a cliff at the edge of the pine forest and are approached by one of the prettiest forest trails on the island. This walk will take you to some of the most secluded and peaceful spots on the island. Several alternative routes are included so you can enjoy this lovely area of Alonnisos many times. The walk is on established paths and is therefore relatively easy.

Follow the 10 km marathon walk until:

with the cisterna in front of you, take the dirt road to the right (ignoring the path downhill to the right which leads to the public spring of Mega Nero). Continue on this road, around a right hand bend, past another road joining from the left and you will come to a T-junction with a wide, surfaced road. Turn left here and almost immediately left again where there is a small fenced-in area of geese, chickens and other assorted wildlife on the right hand side.

Walk down this road and keep left where there is a dirt track off to the right (this dirt track to the right is the direct route to the two churches of Aghii Anarghiri). **This is point 'A' for return reference.**

You will soon arrive at the beach of Tsoukalia, the largest beach on this the south west side of the island. As you approach the beach notice the abundance of pottery shards scattered all about. Behind the broken fence line on the right is where the archaeologists have, in recent years, begun to excavate the site.

> **Pottery pieces have been discovered here which date back to the 4th century BC. Amphorae (pots) were produced here to transport wine by ship to such far away destinations as Black Sea and North African ports. Ships replenished their supply of amphorae here, the broken ones being discarded on the beach, hence the remains visible to this day. Amphorae handles bearing the mark IKION, (taken from Ikos one of the ancient names of Alonnisos) have been found here. Please respect this site and do not remove any items of pottery.**

The windmill on the left of the beach is a new building. When you are ready to move on make your way along the back of the beach to the right and go up to the remains of an old gate above you in the fence line, or what's left of it at that point. This route is now marked by red spots. Go through the gate and continue up slightly to the left and then turn left across the gully which runs down to the beach. As you clear the gully the path leads sharply up to the right under a big old pine tree. The path is red spot marked on a gradual ascent but basically you just need to go straight up the hillside in front of you. There is usually a herd of sheep on this hillside. When you get to the top there are several places amongst the trees at the cliff edge with fabulous views to the north across the bay of Megali Amos and your next destination off to the right, the two churches of Aghii Anarghiri.

With your back to Tsoukalia beach follow the trail to your right along the cliff top. The trail curves around and slightly down to the left and you then turn sharply right up hill across a small bare field. Continue up and you will find the trail again on your right heading between low bushes and then some very large pine trees. You will come to a lovely clearing amongst the trees where you will see many of the pine trees with resin collecting tins attached.

You will also see many nibbled pine cones on the forest floor. There are no squirrels on Alonnisos, the nibbling is done by rats.

On the far side of the clearing you will see a fence with a gate of sorts in it consisting of bits of old rope and wire, but it is easier to simply step over the lowest point of the fence. Continue right on the trail on the other side of the fence and you will quickly come to a junction with a dirt road where you need to turn left. *This is point 'B' for return reference.*

Continue on this dirt road and eventually the road ends at a house on the right. The path continues to the left of the house and up some stone steps, enjoy this lovely section through the forest. After a few minutes you will come to more steps down to your left (just before the steps and on the right note that there is a path which enters the forest line and follows a black pvc water pipe). In early summer you will see and smell lots of wild garlic here. *See return option 2.*

At the top of the steps to the right is a lovely view across the slate roof of the old church and out to sea. As you go down the steps on the right are the remains of the stone walls of the old monastery. At the bottom of the steps on the right is the modern church and a little further on the old church.

Aghii Anarghiri: the churches of the healing Saints, Agios Kosmas and Agios Damianas. The Saints were 4th century Arab doctors who treated the poor in Athens for no charge - Anarghiri means without payment. The old church dates from the 15th - 16th century and has been carefully restored. Formerly there was a monastery on this site and ruins of the cells can still be seen. The newer church was built just after the second world war. There is a lovely wooden bell tower on the cliff edge and notice the large hole in the ground on the side of the old church nearest to you. This is a cisterna or water tank uncovered during renovation work, as were human remains, believed to be the monks who once lived there. This is a fantastic spot to watch the sunset.

Follow the path along the cliff in front of the old church and down through the forest, with wonderful views of the bay of Megali Amos and its beaches. The path keeps close to the cliff and then down to the right of a new house, emerging onto a dirt road. Directly opposite you is the lovely little pebble beach of Tourkoneri. This makes an excellent swim and lunch stop.

From here there are several alternative routes back to Patitiri which you may like to explore another day. See Alternative Return Routes at the end.

This is the main return route. From the beach with your back to the sea, take the forest road up to the left. This is a fairly long uphill section, so pace yourself! At the top turn right and just past the spring on the left look for a path going up on the left, usually marked by a red spot. Follow this path through the forest (there are several fallen trees along this section but they are easy to go around) and you will come out onto a dirt road. Turn right here and follow the road past a stone wall on your left and a turning on the right. After some time, having passed many established cypress trees on your left, the road will bend sharply to the left.

This is a shortcut to omit the pine resin collection point. On the right hand side of the bend is a red spotted optional path which takes you down towards the back of the old goat encampment. The path veers off to the right before this so keep a close watch for the markers. Continue to follow the path down through the forest and you will emerge into an olive grove. Keeping the stone wall on your left continue on the small path until you join a road. Here you turn right and soon pass the entrance to the Homeopathic Academy on your left. Continue as in alternative return route 2.

Follow the road down and you will see below you in the forest to the right a ramshackle old goat encampment. Follow the road to the right and just around this bend to the right in front of the goats you will normally see a large number of cylindrical metal containers. This is the collection point for the resin tapped from the pine trees. Take a look and you will see how it changes from a clear sticky liquid into a hard white candle wax-like substance.

Continue on the same road past this point, ignoring the left turn towards the main asphalt road behind the builder's yard. You will pass the entrance to the International Academy of Classical Homeopathy on your left (if you have an interest in homeopathy you may visit to make enquiries), then on your right the geese etc which you passed earlier. Follow the road around to the left until it meets the main asphalt road. Turn right and follow the road around an S bend, past the turning on the left to Votsi and back into Patitiri.

Alternative Return Routes:

1. The direct route is simply to retrace your steps until reference point 'B'. From here continue straight on until you meet the road to Tsoukalia at reference point 'A'. Turn left up to the junction with the geese etc, turn right (if you then want to visit the public spring at Mega Nero take the second right turn. The spring is about 200m down this track and you can then take the path on the left as you look at the spring to re-join the road you were on) and follow the road around to the left until it meets the main asphalt road. Turn right and follow the road around an 'S' bend, past the turning on the left to Votsi and back into Patitiri.

2: Go back to the church, up the steps and take the small path on the left through the forest which follows the black pvc water pipe. You will emerge in an olive grove, follow the path along the right hand edge of the olive grove and straight on to the forest line (the derelict-looking house is below you to the right). When you reach a forest road, turn right. Keep following the forest road until you come to *a T-junction with another larger dirt road with a stone wall facing you.* Turn right here, follow the road and after some time, having passed many established cypress trees on your left, the road will bend sharply to the left (see **shortcut to omit the pine resin collection point.**). Follow the road down and you will see below you in the forest to the right a ramshackle goat encampment. Now follow the main return route.

3. From the beach, with your back to the sea take the forest road up to the left. This is a fairly long uphill section, so pace yourself! At the top turn right, past the spring on the left (NOTE there are many orchids along the edges of these forest trails, particularly woodcock and bee orchids). Now simply follow the road through the forest until you come to *the T-junction with the stone wall facing* you mentioned in alternative return route 2 above, turn right and proceed as in alternative return route 2.

4. From Tourkoneri beach, with your back to the sea, take the forest road up to the left. This is a fairly long uphill section, pace yourself. At the top turn left (this forest road continues around the coast of Megali Amos) and after a short time you will see a track going up off to the right into the forest as the road bends around to the left. Take the track off to the right and immediately turn right up into an olive grove. Keep to the right and head straight up with the forest line on your right. You will very quickly come to a dirt access track leading off to the left (it may be a bit obscured by long grass), follow this track as it turns right and heads uphill, past a new house being built at time of writing (there are many bee orchids around here). You will pass a blue and white VW van riddled with shotgun pellet holes on the right and then come to T-junction with a main dirt road. Directly in front of you is a new mini development of houses and close to the road on the left are the stone remains of an old church, still visible. The building of these houses was delayed for several years whilst the site was excavated (if you turned left here you would be heading in the direction of the high coast road around Megali Amos or to Kastraki, both of which are described as separate walks). Turn right and continue along the road and after a few minutes the *stone wall at the T-junction* referred to in alternative return route 2 will be on your left. Continue as in alternative return route 2.

South west coast near the Old Village, with the islet of Manolas in the far distance

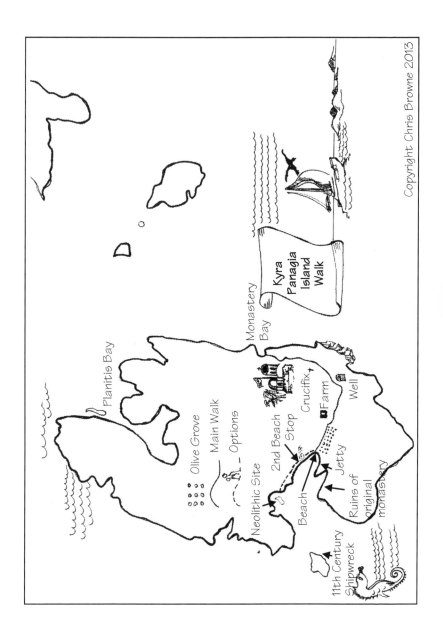

Planitis Bay

Olive Grove

—— Main Walk
--- Options

Monastery
Bay

Neolithic Site

2nd Beach
Stop

Beach

Jetty

Crucifix

Farm

Well

Ruins of
original
monastery

11th Century
Shipwreck

Kyra
Panagia
Island
Walk

Copyright Chris Browne 2013

Kyra Panagia Island Walk

Route: *Monastery – Ayios Petros Bay*

Distance: 4 km

Time: 1.5 hours without stops

Swim Stop: Yes

No Taverna

Walking sandals and shorts ok. Take swimwear.

> Kyra Panagia is the largest of the islands surrounding Alonnisos. Most excursion boats make the same stops on this trip. First at Monastery Bay on the east coast and secondly at Ayios Petros bay in the south-west. If you explain when booking your trip that you would like to do the walk from the monastery to Ayios Petros, and then also have a word with the captain of the boat, most will be accommodating. When you disembark at Monastery Bay make sure you take what you need for the walk as you will not re-join the boat until you reach Ayios Petros bay.

The first part of the walk is up steep concrete steps which turn into a rocky footpath up to the monastery. This is the hardest part of the whole walk. You will walk along the fence line of the monastery garden and then turn left through the old wooden gate. Through the gate there is a cisterna with a water tap on the right and the garden on the left. Notice the old WWII mine casing in the garden. Walk straight ahead and on the right is the door into the monastery courtyard. You will either be given a short guided tour of the monastery or be left to look around on your own.

If left to your own devices, this post-Byzantine monastery dates from the 12th century, was restored in 1905 and renovated in 1992. The name Kyra Panagia means "The Virgin Mary". The monastery is dedicated to the birth of Mary and owned and administered by the monastery of Meghisti Lavra on Mount Athos, the garden of Mary. Nowadays there is normally only one caretaker monk in residence. The remains of an earlier 6/7th century church were discovered on the site of the existing church inside the courtyard during renovation work. When you go through the door into the courtyard there are shawls hanging on the left for women to use who are not appropriately dressed (bare shoulders and legs). The church is just ahead and to the left of a lovely cobbled floor. Stand looking into the church door, slightly right of centre, with your back against the wall behind you. Formed in the cobbles is the year the floor was laid. See if you can find it (1908). Outside the church there is a sign over the door which translates as "Welcome the Virgin Bride of God". There is also a shaped length of wood hanging horizontally on which a mallet was rhythmically banged to summon the monks to prayer. If you go around the church anti-clockwise the rooms you pass on your right are first the old bakery, then the olive mill, the olive press, and just outside the door the tank where the grapes were turned into wine. There is a wonderful viewing platform up a flight of stairs, from where the Greek and yellow and black Byzantine flags normally fly. The double-headed eagle on the Byzantine flag represents the split between Orthodoxy and Catholicism following the schism in the 13th century, one head looking east, one head looking west. The flag's yellow background is a symbol of peace; in times of conflict this changed to red.

Note: The old footpath described below is being widened into a road.

When you have finished in the monastery go out of the gate and turn immediately left and sharply uphill (not the level track on the left which goes to the well).

Now simply follow the track and stop every now and again to appreciate the view back to the monastery. You will come to a left hand bend where there is some of the only shade along the way, a good place to rest. Continue on up and take a right turn, beyond which you will lose the view back to the monastery. The next landmark you will come to is the large crucifix which marks the high point of the footpath. Now it is metal but used to be a simple wooden cross supported by a cairn of stones. Continue on the path which now starts to descend. At the bottom turn right where there is a well with a padlocked cover in front of you and a stone trough. You now begin to walk through olive groves, some of the olive trees being the broadest, and therefore the oldest, on the islands.

The path now divides and you should take the right fork which leads slightly uphill towards the farmhouse and outbuildings. The path bears left in front of the farm.

The path now becomes a road and you continue on down with fenced olive groves to your left until you emerge at the first pebble beach of Ayios Petros bay.

To the right of the beach the path continues along the edge of the bay until you come to an olive grove.

As you walk along this path look across the bay to your left and on top of the first headland you will see the stone remains of the original Byzantine monastery of Kyra Panagia, believed to date from the 6/7th century.

Continue through the olive grove and on your left a lovely white pebble beach will soon appear. This is the usual point where excursion boats make their second and longest stop for swimming and lunch at anchor. They would normally collect you from the beach in their tender.

If you walk across the beach the path does continue around the bay, firstly close to the sea and then slightly uphill to the right until it drops down towards a tiny islet deep inside a small cove within the main bay. A Neolithic settlement (c6000-5000BC) was excavated on this islet some years ago and is believed to be the oldest known settlement in the Aegean Sea.

"Saint Simeon the God-receiver" carries Jesus as
an infant in his arms (Luke 2:25-32)

Peristera Island Walk

Main Route: *Ksilo(Vasiliko Bay) – Vouni – Peristera – Peristeri Bay*

Distance: 6 kms

Time: 3-4 hours without stops

Swim Stop: Yes

No Tavernas

Walking sandals and shorts are ok for most of the route but take long trousers or zip-offs as there are some scratchy bits. Take swimwear.

Outside of some limited seasonal occupation to work the olive groves and fish, Peristera is now a deserted island although it did once have a permanent population. Peristera means "dove". The route for this walk is not marked and is therefore a bit more difficult to follow than most. However, it is one of the most rewarding and provides wonderful views of Alonnisos. If you follow the instructions carefully and refer to the photographs taken en route you should have no problem. You can reach Peristera by hiring your own boat, by speaking to the fishermen at Steni Vala or Captain Panayotis of the "Stella" pleasure boat from Patitiri.

The walk starts from "Ksilo" which is on the right hand side of Vasiliko (basil) bay as you enter it. Steni Vala is the closest point on Alonnisos.

At "Ksilo" you will see a small house close to the shore which belongs to the Mavrikis family from Steni Vala, also owners of the museum in Patitiri. To the left of the house is a small beach and directly below it a small jetty. This is where your walk starts. Follow the path up from the jetty and to the right of the house. Walk up the slope (past a new stone built cottage) with the sea to your right. You will come to a paved aloni (threshing floor),

119

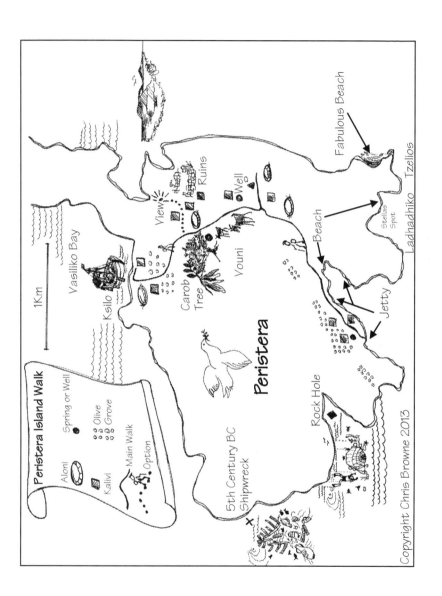

Peristera Island Walk

Aloni

Kalivi

Spring or Well

Olive Grove

Main Walk

Option

Vasiliko Bay

1Km

Ksilo

View

Ruins

Well

Carob Tree

Vouni

Beach

Stellas Spot

Ladhadhiko   Tzelios

Fabulous Beach

Jetty

Peristera

Rock Hole

5th Century BC Shipwreck

one of several you will see on your walk. With your back to the sea take the path straight in front of you which goes uphill. There are quite a few tracks which cross on this hillside but follow the one which goes left and up across the hillside, past many old almond trees. The house where you started should now be below you to the left. At the far side of the almond grove the path continues up to the right along a deep cut in the ground made by rainwater. Follow this to the top of the rise (it is worth stopping every now and again along this section to take in the ever changing views across Vasiliko bay and back to the coast of Alonnisos), where you will be amongst low cistus bushes, and then down to the right towards a big olive tree at the bottom. Past the olive tree the path goes sharply uphill again through low cistus bushes. You then come to a section where you will be walking among large strawberry trees, along obvious water courses at some times and on up to emerge at an unpaved aloni with a few tumble down buildings off to your left. To the extreme left are the remains of a low stone animal pen, walk along the right hand side of this, then up and carefully left over the rocks and simply enjoy the view north out to the marine park.

From the aloni take the path to the right and straight ahead along a short relatively flat section, then down to the left at the end and up to your right you will come to a spring. The water trickles from the rock face in front of you beneath the largest carob tree I have seen. There are goats, mules, donkeys and even a horse from time to time on Peristera and they all beat a path here to drink. If you look back from here to where you have just come from you will see several derelict cottages. With the spring on your right take the path straight ahead. To your left is a fenced area. From here the path is simple to follow and reasonably level. After some time you will see in the distance a flat area with cypress pines at the top of a rise in the path. This is your next destination. When you reach this small field, with a little cottage on the left, there is a large bush in the centre, in front of you and slightly to the left. Under the bush is a well and to the right near the olive tree wild peppermint proliferates in spring.

Continue on the path out of this field and over a low terrace wall and you will see above you to the left a concrete trig point. This is your next destination. Follow the path uphill and you will come to a 'roundabout' on your left formed by a large bush with a path around it. Turn left here and at the top you will come to another aloni with the trig point on your left. Again, there are fabulous 360 degree views. On the way back down on your left just opposite the 'roundabout' there is a small path through the trees to a cottage in a reasonable state of repair if you would like to take a look.

This is a good point to turn around if you have left your boat at Ksilo. If you have arranged to be picked up from the end of the walk, or if you intend to do the whole walk there and back, (Brrrravo! if you do), then having come downhill to the 'roundabout' turn left. Follow the path downhill and slightly to the right and you soon come to another aloni. All around here are ruined dwellings. The path continues straight across the aloni and past an area of bare reddish earth on the right. This is a good time to put on your 'legs' if you have zip-offs, or long trousers as the undergrowth can be a bit scratchy from here. Continue on the path as it continues gradually downhill, there are some great views to the south east coast of Alonnisos from this section of the walk, with Kokkino Kastro prominent in the foreground. The path is fairly clear but as a landmark there is one point where the path turns left and down to a large strawberry tree on the left. At the strawberry tree you turn right and you will come to a small shed on your left at the start of a small open area. Go straight across the open area and look for the path again in the low bushes. From here the undergrowth is normally very closed in across the path.

The path now begins to wind sharply downhill and you will reach a point where it looks as though you are going to have to go straight down a bare ravine in front of you. Don't worry! The path turns left here and continues down until you come to a big olive tree at the bottom of a small gully, which is the end of the ravine you passed earlier. Go straight across the gully and left out the other side and follow the lower path with the stone wall on your right straight ahead through the olive grove.

After a couple of minutes on your left there is a way down and out onto the beach at the back of Peristeri bay.

At the end of the olive grove Peristeri bay is below you to the left and going down to the left by the last olive tree is a steep path which winds down to a small cottage right on the shore. This cottage has a small jetty where a boat can tie up.

From the end of the olive grove the path bears right through low bushes and follows the coast. Eventually you will come to a gate across the path, beyond which are olive groves. Please shut the gate behind you. The next section is a delightful walk as the path takes you around the coast and past several kalivis (cottages). There are several tracks but simply follow the coast around. Eventually, where there are two kalivis slightly above you and to the right, the path drops down to your left towards the coast past a well and a large prickly pear plant. Just below this the main path leads you down to the jetty or if you turn right and then left at a large pine tree you will come down to the small beach.

Quarry

Field

Polemika

Prasso

Mooring

Skantzoura

Skantili

Dio Adelphia

(The Two Brothers)

Ostria

Skantzoura

- ◼ Farm House
- ● Well or Spring
- ○ Aloni
- ⛪ Monastery

Copyright Chris Browne 2013

124

Skantzoura Island Walk

Route: *Up to the monastery, farmhouse, aloni (threshing floor) and back.*

Optional walk to the disused marble quarry.

Distance: 3 kms

Time: 1.5 hours up and down without stops.

Optional walk is around an extra 5 kms there and back.

Swim Stop: Yes

No Taverna

Walking shoes and long trousers recommended. Take swimwear.

The rarely visited island of Skantzoura with its shores of white marble, and the nearby island of Polemika, are an important habitat for the rare Audouin's gull and the Eleonora's falcon. There is also a forest of low Juniper trees. The last monk, brother Nimnos, left in the 1960's and the island is now deserted. There is an old church and ruined monastery named Evangelistria (The Immaculate Conception) and a derelict farmhouse. There are goats put on the island to graze from time to time.

Skantzoura is about 12 miles from Patitiri. From Patitiri it is possible to go through the channel between the islands of Dio Adelphia (The Two Brothers). I have been many times to Skantzoura with captain Panayotis and his father Pantezese of the "Stella" pleasure boat from Patitiri, it is a unique place and my favourite island. A swim followed by lunch sat on the flat marble shore is a delight.

As you approach the island from Alonnisos you can see a building about mid-centre on top of the island. This is the old farmhouse with the church and monastery nearby. Directly below the farmhouse is a small bay, the shores of which are made up of huge flat slabs of marble. Head straight into this bay and you will see directly in front of you an area of the shore which is unlike the rest, being made of much smaller stones (this was caused by the Greek navy using the island for target practice, thankfully it only happened the once). Immediately to the left of this is a flat landing area on the rocks with a couple of mooring poles where you can tie up. This bay is a fabulous place for snorkelling with many large fish and moray eels and fan mussels growing from the sea bed.

With your back to the sea head straight up from the landing area, over the rocks and follow the path as it bears slightly to the right. You quickly meet a small path joining from the left (**reference point** A).

South East Alonnisos, with the Two Brothers and the island of Skantzoura in the far distance

126

Keep right here and follow the path up (long trousers are recommended as the undergrowth closes in a bit). You will come to a sharp left hand bend in a relatively open patch of undergrowth. Take a moment here to admire the view back to Dio Adelphia with Alonnisos beyond, Peristera to the right and Skopelos to the left. You are surrounded by juniper and strawberry trees here. Continue up and after about 20m the path turns sharp right and continues uphill. Shortly after you make this turn you will walk over many large crystals, mostly quartzite, embedded in the path. At the top the path bears to the left and you will come to an area of relatively open fields with buildings in front of you.

These fields are called "Lakka" and wheat was grown in them. You will see the aloni or threshing floor used to winnow the wheat later in the walk.

The building to your right is the old farmhouse and to your left is a storage area built around a well-head, with the church and monastery behind. **WARNING!** The buildings are in a VERY poor state of repair due to neglect and recent earthquakes so for your own safety keep well away and **DO NOT ENTER.**

Looking back out to sea towards Alonnisos, look down and across to your right and you will see a very large bare field formed by a natural bowl in the island. On the far side of this field is an olive grove and beyond it to the north an area of white rocks. This is the old marble quarry and you can walk there later if you wish.

Stand in between the buildings with the farmhouse on your right and walk straight ahead, past the storage building on your left. Continue past the next entrance on the left which goes into the small church and past another outbuilding.

On your left there is now a small field slightly above you from which there is a wonderful view back to the monastery, farmhouse and beyond. The path continues to the right, past a few tumbledown animal pens on the right and alongside a derelict outbuilding on the left. With this outbuilding immediately on your left follow the path between the bushes for a few meters and you will come to an old paved aloni (threshing floor), with the pole to which the donkey or mule was tethered to pull the stone grinding wheel still in place. From here there is a magnificent view to all the islands of the Marine Park, plus Skopelos, Evia and Skyros.

Look back towards Alonnisos, turn right and you can walk down to another small field. Keep right across the field towards a single large tree, next to which is a walled water collection hole. The tree is an oriental plane tree.

Return the way you came down to **reference point A**. To return to the boat continue down or turn right here to explore further to the disused marble quarry.

To get to the quarry turn right at reference point A and follow this path around and down to the right until you come out at one end of the open field you saw from above. Turn left (take a good look behind you and mark the path you entered from for your return) and walk straight across the field, you will pass a well off to your left.

> *You will almost certainly come across large brass shell casings on the ground. These are from flares left over from the same military exercises which saw the small part of the coastline in the bay destroyed.*

At the far end of the field look to your right and follow the obvious path up towards the olive trees. You will eventually emerge in open ground and see the old quarry below you to the left with a few derelict buildings around it. Directly opposite you is the islet of Polemika. The sea creates the most beautiful colours where it washes over the marble shore.

Return the same way to the bay. On the way back towards Alonnisos there is another fabulous snorkelling site on the extreme left hand side of the Two Brothers as you approach. The left of the two islets is the "Big Brother" and on the extreme left of this is a beautiful secluded cove called "Ostria", or southerly. Just off the end of the island there is a large rocky outcrop, and between the two of them a reef populated by many different species of fish. In calm seas, if you swim from inside the cove around the rocky outcrop, you will experience a dramatic change in sea depth.

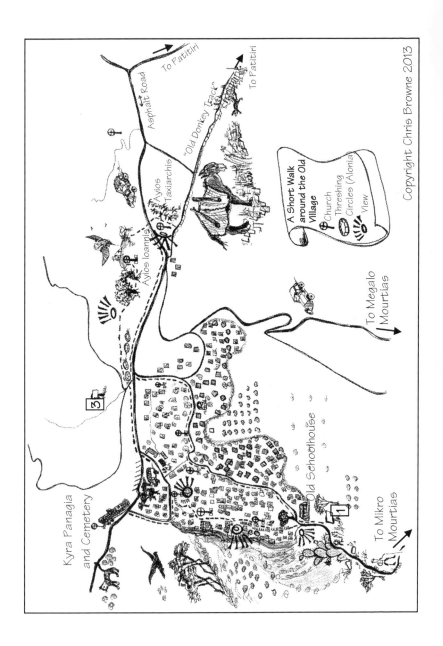

To Patitiri

To Patitiri

Asphalt Road

"Old Donkey Track"

A Short Walk around the Old Village

✝ Church

Threshing Circles (Alonia)

View

Copyright Chris Browne 2013

Ayios Taxiarchis

Ayios Ioannis

To Megalo Mourtias

3

Kyra Panagia and Cemetery

Old Schoolhouse

1

To Mikro Mourtias

130

A Short Walk Around the Old Village

Distance: 3.5 kms

Time: 1.5 hours

Swim Stop: No

Tavernas & Cafes: Yes

Walking sandals and shorts are ok.

> This walk will take you on a leisurely circuit around and through the Old Village to the best viewpoints, churches and places of interest.

Start at the bus stop opposite Taverna Panselinos and walk down the main road towards Patitiri. On your left you will quickly come to the "Alonia" (threshing circles), walk up the stone steps to your left and follow the path along. Stop from time to time to admire the wild flowers here in spring, the views across both sides of the island and the rather bizarre TV aerials fixed to a rock belonging to a house below you to the right! To your left you will look down to the small bays of Vrisitsa and Yalia, and out to the islet of Manolas and the rock of Stavros (crucifix). On a clear day Mount Athos is visible over the top of Manolas and Mount Olympus further to the left.

Continue along the path and on your right you will see the small 18th century church of Ayios Ioannis, the entrance to which is framed by a large holly oak tree forming an archway. The church is sadly locked but this spot is a great place to watch and listen to the Bee Eaters in the summer. Carry on past the church keeping to the left of the large rock with the crucifix on the top until you come to a metal gate. Go around the gate, cross the road and turn left downhill. Immediately on your right turn up the concrete driveway and right again on a small signposted path to the

131

church of Ayios Taxiarchis. The church is surrounded by rosemary for remembrance and is a wonderfully peaceful place with lovely views to the Old Village and Skopelos.

Return to the road and turn left back up towards the Old Village. On your left you will pass the end of the "Old Donkey Track" and then the turning to Megalos Mourtias.

Continue on up the main road and take the first entrance into the old village on the left (opposite the "Alonia"). Follow the plaka road and just a short distance along on the right is a small private church belonging to the eco-friendly new villas above built by Dieter & Ziggy. Continue along the plaka road and turn right at a small fork in the road, the area down to the left is known locally as "Little England". Continue along and you will go past a well on your left, this is a municipal well built in 1887 and nearby on the right is the 18th century church of Ayios Evangelismos (the church of the Immaculate Conception).

Continue along and take a small turning to your right and then immediately left, still following the main street. On your right you will see a house with a small pebble design inset into its front wall. Notice how small some of the doors are along here.

Keep right up the steps past no. 62 and at the end turn left by the fig tree and a blue door on the right, this leads down to the old primary school, built in 1903. Take the steps down to the right of the school and stop to admire the view: this is the start of the footpath down to Mikros Mourtias beach. Return to the fig tree and take the steep steps straight up passing the 16th/17th century church of Ayios Dimitrios on your right just before the top. Turn left at the top, next to the Paraport (little door) taverna and take in the views at the end. You can see Kalovoulos peak opposite, Skopelos island and the tiny beach of Mikros Mourtias below you.

Turn around and walk back along this relatively level street to the Kastro taverna. Above you and to the left, this section is well worth exploring: you will find the Byzantine castle fortress and the 16/17th century church of Ayios Yorgos. Next to the Kastro taverna is the entrance to an old traditional house museum and just beyond that down a few steps is the small terrace of Plateia Heroon next to a war memorial (the memorial commemorates the 15th August 1944 when 9 local Greek men were shot in reprisal by the German army during the festival of Panagia). From here there are wonderful panoramic views out across the old village. Continue down the cobbled steps, past the church of Ayios Christos with its unique internal mezzanine gallery for women. Across the plateia is the church of Ayios Athanasios and a war memorial commemorating the Balkan wars of 1912/1913. Continue left out of the plateia, past house no. 183, to the junction with the main road. To your left is the island cemetery and the church of Kyra Panagia and a short distance along to your right the bus stop, from where you started your walk.

Cactus in bloom behind the old schoolhouse in the Old Village

Chris founded Alonnisos Walking Club in 2005 with the aim of encouraging both residents and visitors alike to better appreciate and enjoy this outstanding island environment. Since 1996 Chris has guided walks and boat trips around Alonnisos and the islands of the marine park, helping to open up the traditional footpaths which later became the waymarked hiking trails. Before settling on Alonnisos, Chris worked for many years in the Middle East and Africa and has trekked in South America twice to raise money for the Teenage Cancer Trust of the UK. He has also explored the Western Ghats mountain range of southern India on foot and studied yoga there. When not walking or kayaking, in the evenings Chris can very often be found in one of the local tavernas or public spaces entertaining visitors and locals as part of the popular local rock and roll group, the Aloni Band, or as half of the 'Barefoot Blues' duo. He is also an active member of the newly formed island drama group, the Greek Island Thespians (GITs).